# Everyday Christianity, *Every Day*

# Everyday Christianity, *Every Day*

Struggling. Seeking. Succeeding.

**CHAD STAFKO**

*Everyday Christianity, Every Day*
Copyright © 2024 by Kaio Publications
http://www.kaiopublications.org

All rights reserved. No part of this publication may be reproduced, stored in a retrieval system, or transmitted in any form by any means, electronic, mechanical, photocopy, recording, or otherwise, without the prior permission of the author, except as provided for by USA copyright law.

Printed in the United States of America

Scripture taken from the New King James Version®. Copyright © 1982 by Thomas Nelson. Used by permission. All rights reserved. All biblical passages, unless otherwise noted, are from this translation.

ISBN ISBN: 978-1-952955-50-1

Cover and interior design: Marc Whitaker / MTWdesign.net
Typesetting: PerfecType / Nashville, Tennessee
Copyediting and Proofing: Marissa Wold Uhrina, Minneapolis, Minnesota

To my wife Heather—
*you have an incredible faith and mean the world to me.
I couldn't love a person more.*

To my sons, Tyler and Camden—
*may you grow up to be faithful children of God
and be great examples to others.*

To my friend and publisher Clay Young—
*without your vision and inspiration,
this book wouldn't have seen the light of day.*

# Contents

Introduction .................................................................... ix

Chapter One
Let's Start from Scratch ................................................... 1

Chapter Two
God: Where It All Begins .................................................. 9

Chapter Three
Jesus: How It Can Happen ............................................... 17

Chapter Four
So, There's This Family I Know . . . ................................. 25

Chapter Five
You Gotta Love Our Father .............................................. 31

Chapter Six
You Gotta Love Each Other ............................................. 39

Chapter Seven
The Quality You Must Have ............................................ 47

Chapter Eight
What Can I Do? ................................................................ 55

Chapter Nine
So, You're a Billboard ...................................................... 63

Chapter Ten
It's Not If You Fail but When You Fail ..................................................... 71

Chapter Eleven
LOOK + LOOK + DO = SUCCESS ....................................................... 79

Chapter Twelve
Everyday Christianity—The Extraordinary Life ................................... 87

Chapter Thirteen
It Will Be Worth It All .............................................................................. 95

# Introduction

First, this book is practical, designed to guide, motivate, and challenge you, your way of life, and your perception of what comprises the everyday Christian life. Each chapter ends with a challenge task. It is my hope that you will find each one beneficial. Some may not be difficult, while others may require a radical shift in your mentality. Regardless, each challenge will help you draw closer to the Almighty God. I ask you to take each challenge task seriously since each will attempt to make the idea in the chapter practical.

Second, keep your Bible close by because we will refer to it often. The words of the Bible that sit on your nightstand or in your living room are "God-breathed" (2 Tim. 3:16). The Word of God is powerful and—if you allow it—will change your life like no other book. There is no other book written, or that will ever be written, that approaches the wisdom and insight into God and what He wants out of us in this life. We will consider a number of biblical passages, which I ask you to think about, meditate on, and ultimately act on. Underline, highlight, or somehow mark verses in your Bible. Please do not just read this book and take what I say for granted. Keep God's Word close to you and rely on it.

All that said, let's begin with a question as we start from scratch to have everyday Christianity—every single day. What kind of Christian do you want to be?

# Chapter 1

# Let's Start from Scratch

I have no sense of direction. People who always seem to know which way is north or know how to get from somewhere to anywhere amaze me. Name a town close to where I live or where I grew up, and there is an excellent chance that I have been lost in it. I have even been lost more times than I care to mention in parking garages. Those maps in amusement parks and at the mall that have a "you are here" sticker on them are a godsend for people like me. And GPS? That was seemingly created for people like me. Being lost is no fun and quite frustrating regardless of the situation.

Remember as a kid sitting in math class wrangling over how to solve a math problem? It was an empty feeling when you looked around and everyone else had finished while you asked yourself why all your classmates seemed to know how to solve the problem. You wished you could just start from scratch, but even then, you wondered where to start in order to solve the problem. I've been there. Again, more times than I prefer to reveal here.

This same feeling of helplessness can occur in a spiritual sense. You sit in church services and look around. It appears as though everyone else has their lives figured out. (Not all of us do, but we hide it well.) They nod their heads in approval when the minister speaks and sing each hymn with fervor. They seem to be great Christians living a productive and happy life with a faith that appears to be impenetrable by Satan.

And there you sit, just like in math class, wondering how you could do the same. You want to have this same kind and measure of faith, but you wonder if you missed a step somewhere along life's journey. Well, let me assure you that you can be all that you have ever wanted to be as a Christian regardless of where you are in your Christian walk. New Christian, seasoned Christian, or those in between, I ask you to simply start from scratch with me and become an everyday Christian every single day.

## The Equation for Extraordinary

Now understand something: when we use the term *everyday Christian*, we're not talking about being ordinary. We are talking about being extraordinary by being the type of Christian that God wants us to be in every aspect of our lives day after day. We want to develop a degree of faith in God that is unquenchable by the fiery darts of Satan. We want to develop a level of dedication and commitment to following God that will not be swayed despite what is thrown at us in this life. We want to be everything God wants us to be. We want to make our Father in heaven proud. Every single person, regardless of current circumstances, can become an everyday Christian every single day of life.

We are going down this path together, small step after small step. Remember the old Chinese proverb, "A journey of a thousand miles begins with a single step." That is exactly what we are going to do. Think of some one-word characteristics that describe how you want to be as a

Christian. Go ahead and brainstorm for a few moments. Close the book and think about this question. No, really, please. Close this book; close your eyes; just think. Now, jot down the words that came to mind in the margins of this page. Here are some that you may or may not have written down: loving, compassionate, faithful, joyful, kind, passionate, forgiving, patient, gentle.

You can have all of these and other Christian qualities, but it takes effort from you. Obtaining any of these characteristics does not happen by accident. Everyday Christianity takes effort as does anything that has value. Nobody has ever accidentally stumbled upon great faith, an unrelenting zeal for Christ, or any other Christian characteristic. Those people you know who have a rock-solid faith were not just born that way. It took effort on their part.

> *Nobody has ever accidentally stumbled upon great faith, an unrelenting zeal for Christ, or any other Christian characteristic.*

Just reading this book or even reading the Bible cover to cover does not translate to automatically having these qualities. There are some hands-on processes that need to be learned. In the same way that I, as a mechanically challenged person, cannot simply read a detailed parts manual and fix an engine, we cannot just read the Bible, and—*poof!*—we are now the most dedicated Christian to walk the planet. However, the Bible does give us the formula to success in living the Christian life. You will find reference to the following passage several times throughout this book. Consider what James, the brother of Jesus, wrote in James 1:22, 25: "But be doers of the word, and not hearers only, deceiving yourselves. . . . But he who looks into the perfect law of liberty and continues *in it*, and is not a forgetful hearer but a doer of the work, this one will be blessed in what he does."

Did you notice an equation in this verse? If you can put this verse to memory, and practice it, you will be pressing the accelerator toward the path upon which God wants you. Everyday Christianity is hearing what God says for us to do and then doing it every day. Put it in an equation form: $E=MC^2$. Just kidding. Here's the real thing:

Look into the Bible + Continue looking into it + Remember what it says + Act upon what you read = God's blessings upon you.

LOOK + LOOK + DO = SUCCESS

Yes, it's that simple. And quite frankly, everyday Christianity is a lifestyle every one of us can have every single day, no matter your circumstances. That's right! Don't believe me? Then let me briefly introduce you a group of folks and an individual who accomplished just that.

## You Can Change!

Back in Bible times there was a town that was the epitome of immorality: Corinth. Corinth was a town of great wealth, importance, and sophistication. With that came a host of immoral distractions and destructive ways of life. Sound like anywhere you live today? Amazingly enough, the church found its way there. And it was not as if some "good" folks were transplanted there, and they just existed as this small group of lifelong good people living in a city of great sin. No, they were far from it. The very folks who made up this congregation had lived quite a life of sin, but something inside of them changed. The people who made up the church in Corinth changed in an extraordinary manner.

Notice how they are described in 1 Corinthians 6:9–11:

> Do you not know that the unrighteous will not inherit the kingdom of God? Do not be deceived. Neither fornicators, nor idolaters, nor adulterers, nor homosexuals, nor sodomites, nor thieves, nor covetous, nor drunkards, nor revilers, nor extortioners will inherit the kingdom of God. And such were some of you. But you were washed, but you were sanctified, but you were justified in the name of the Lord Jesus and by the Spirit of our God.

Friends, that is change, real change, a 180-degree turn from their prior lives.

> *The man who wrote the most books of the Bible was not always a friend of God and was far from a friend to Jesus. In fact, he was the chief enemy of Jesus Christ and the disciples, but he changed.*

You may not be nearly as "evil" as were many of the Corinthians, or perhaps you have committed some of those same sins or even are currently struggling with one or more of those sins. Regardless, they changed and became everyday Christians, and so can you. Now, to that individual I mentioned earlier. The man who wrote the most books of the Bible was not always a friend of God and was far from a friend to Jesus. In fact, he was the chief enemy of Jesus Christ and the disciples, but he changed. And oh, how he changed! Saul was a great persecutor of Christians. When I say "persecutor," I am not talking about making fun or making life a little difficult for the followers of Christ. Saul killed Christians and was present when the first recorded Christian martyr, Stephen, was killed. By all accounts Saul was a bad man.

One day Saul had an encounter with Jesus Christ on the road to Damascus, and eventually, he converted to Christianity (Acts 9). He also changed his name to Paul. That is right: the apostle Paul, who was arguably the greatest ambassador for Christ the world has ever known, lived much of his life opposite of how God wanted him to live. Thus, he had to change, and it took effort on his part. He wrote in Philippians 3:7–9,

> But what things were gain to me, these I have counted loss for Christ. Yet indeed I also count all things loss for the excellence of the knowledge of Christ Jesus my Lord, for whom I have suffered the loss of all things, and count them as rubbish, that I may gain Christ and be found in Him, not having my own righteousness, which is from the law, but that which is through faith in Christ, the righteousness which is from God by faith . . .

Did you catch that? Paul said he "lost all things." In other words, he started from scratch, and he essentially said his old life was of no value. By most accounts, his life was quite valuable. He was extremely well-educated and powerful. When Saul walked down the street, people noticed. And those "Christians," well, if Paul told them to jump, they had best ask, "How high?" Saul commanded respect, was no doubt wealthy, and was certainly greatly respected. He had it all, didn't he? Some would say absolutely. He had fame, fortune, power. The list could go on.

What does that tell me? Well, it tells me that Saul eventually realized that a life absent of Jesus Christ is a life that is, quite frankly, missing what is most important. Saul was not the first person, nor will he be the last, to realize that power, wealth, and influence are not the treasures of life. Recall what Soloman said of such quests in Ecclesiastes 12:8, "Vanity of vanities. All *is* vanity."

So, if a man who was Public Enemy #1 of Jesus Christ could change, and a group of individuals who lived in the Sin Capital of the region could change, you can too. It is possible and can be done with great dedication. But just like Paul and the Corinthians, change took effort, and it will with you also as you seek to become an everyday Christian every day. You can do it! You can change!

**CHALLENGE #1:** ❖❖❖❖❖❖❖

Read James 1:22–25 several times over the next twenty-four hours. Then, as the verse says, use what God has said in those few words as a mirror for your life. Do you follow the "equation" found therein? Think about it! Seriously ask yourself that question.

# Chapter 2

# God: Where It All Begins

What motivates you? Motivation is what drives us to do most everything, from the smallest of choices to the most complex of decisions. Consider the simple task of brushing your teeth. Even though it's a simple activity, it requires motivation to complete. There are two motivations that cause me to brush my teeth each morning. The first, a long-term motivation, is that I want to keep my teeth as long as possible, and regular brushing contributes to healthy teeth. However, that is my secondary motivation. My parents both had healthy teeth into their sixties, and I figure, Lord willing, that there is a good chance I too will have my teeth when I reach that age. My primary motivation is to not have bad breath. As I interact with people on a daily basis, I don't want to "blow away" anyone by my repugnant breath. Not too many folks want to have a conversation with someone whose breath reeks. Brushing my teeth removes my "morning breath." This motivation drives me to get out my toothbrush and toothpaste every single morning.

Realizing our motivation, whether trivial or important, is critical to understand.

## What Is Your Motivation?

OK, so we know that motivation is the fuel that powers results no matter the situation, whether physical or spiritual. Motivation plays an increasingly larger role in a more complex task or decision. Consider the importance of motivation in these aspects of life.

*Why do I want to marry him/her?* She's pretty. He's handsome. She's rich. He's tough. She's a great person. He will make me a better person.

*Why do I want my child in this activity?* It will help him socialize. Maybe this will show her talent.

*Why do I want to be a part of this church?* Services are short, so I have more time. The people there are great. The Bible is their standard. It will help me in my work.

*Why do I want to join this social club?* This is THE club to be in. Maybe I'll meet that special someone. It's involved in an activity I enjoy.

*Why do I want to give my time for church-sponsored ministries?* People will applaud me. It might give me some "grace" from God, so I can do what I want sometimes.

*Why do I want to live and work in this town?* It's close to the city. The restaurants are fabulous. The school system is top-notch.

*Why do I want to follow Christ?* He died to take away the punishment of sin. That's how I was brought up. Jesus treated people nicely, so will I.

These are all motivations. I'm not saying that all are wise motivations, though some are. However, all of them are potential drivers of a specific action or decision. Motivation is of the utmost importance in the Christian life. It is absolutely critical. If your motivation is out of place, at some point you will lose the drive to perform the task, or you may make a poor decision with long-term consequences. If your motivation in service to God and others is to be seen by men and receive accolades, then when the applause fades and disappears, you will quit. If that's the case, you've missed it. You have missed the whole basis for loving God and loving your fellow man.

That said, please read this carefully with the deepest consideration and honesty. Christianity is all about motivation. It may be hard to hear, but consider it specifically in relation to your own life. The primary reason Christians do not live as everyday Christians every day is because they are not motivated to do so. Put another way, the level of your spiritual motivation is directly proportional to the degree to which you love God.

The more you love God, the more you value what He has done for you, and the more you want to live your life for Him.

> *Motivation is of the utmost importance in the Christian life. It is absolutely critical.*

The more you love God, the more motivated you are to serve Him and do what He says for you to do in this life. The more you love God, the more you know that you are no different than the drunk person laying against the building, the man who hits his wife, or the mother who has abandoned her children. They are sinners, and so are you. You cannot get to heaven any more than these people without God. You need God. He does not need you. He wants you to realize that. You need Him; you need Him more than anyone or anything on this earth. (See Rom. 3:23.)

Think about that. Wrestle with it for a moment. Let it percolate in your heart and stir within you. Lay your life alongside that idea of motivation and appraise yourself and your level of motivation: the degree to which you love God and appreciate what He has done for you. Now, just because an individual lacks motivation does not mean he or she is a bad person. Let's be honest, we've all been there before to some extent. Maybe you have not felt motivated to attend church services regularly, to get involved in any church-sponsored activities, or to volunteer for the cause of Christ in some capacity. It happens; we are human. The world distracts us from what is most important in life. Satan knows that he has a large portion of the world in his hands. But those Christians have eluded him, and he is more than happy to try to eliminate or reduce their motivation to serve Almighty God.

## Keeping the Faith

A relevant question now is when I do have a lack in motivation, how do I deal with it?

Let's start with what our motivation should be: God and Jesus. We will look at Jesus in the next chapter. Now let us focus on our Father in heaven, Almighty God. You might wonder how God can be a motivation. To which I now ask you and want you to consider, how can God not be a motivation? Put another way, how can God's love not be enough motivation to live every single day for Him?

Go back with me to the first book of the Bible, Genesis. In 1:26–27, we find these provocative words: "Let Us make man in Our image, according to Our likeness . . . So God created man in His *own* image; in the image of God He created him . . ." Note the link here. God has a vested interest in every person who has or will ever walk this earth, including you, because no matter who you are or what your circumstances are in life, you are a creation of God and are made in His image! Black hair, blond hair, blue hair, white skin, brown skin—it is no matter. You are made in the image of the Creator of the universe!

## God's Interested in You

From the time that God said these words and throughout the entire Old Testament, we see God interested in His people and providing for them. From Noah to Abraham to Joseph to Moses to the Israelite people, and down through the times of the Minor Prophets, there is not the slightest of doubts that God was with His people. That assurance has not changed and will not change in any way, shape, or form from now until the triumphant return of Jesus Christ. If you don't believe me, consider these beautiful words penned in 1 Peter 3:12: "For the eyes of the LORD are on the righteous, And His ears *are* open to their prayers." Please do not gloss over this verse and its awe-inspiring thoughts. Almighty God is interested in you, not in a casual manner, but in the most sincere and deepest of ways. Like a mother who watches over her child in a sea of children, God looks about this earth at His people. He sees our raw emotions, struggles, joys, and heartaches.

God is not the old man-type figure that He appears to be sometimes in movies or on television. He is not the clock master who sets the clock and whatever happens after that is just the way it goes. That is as far from the biblical description of God as there could be.

God is interested in _____. (Put your name in the blank.) The same God who exclaimed, "Let there be light" is the same God that cares about why you are hurting. The same God who parted the Red Sea through His messenger Moses is concerned about your children. The same God who saved poor Jonah from being the lunch of the great fish is the same God who can deliver you from the most difficult of circumstances. And the same God who did not spare the most precious of possessions, His Son, is the same God who considers your spiritual condition to be of paramount and eternal importance.

While it is a familiar passage to most, the words found in John 3:16–17 are some of the most beautiful in all the Scriptures, "For God so loved the world that He gave His only begotten Son, that whoever believes in Him should not perish but have everlasting life. For God did not send His Son into the world to condemn the world, but that the world through Him might be saved." God could have sent His Son for the purpose of only judging the world. He could have sent Him as a measuring stick by which all mankind would be measured and subsequently would fail miserably. Sending Jesus to earth could have provided justice. Instead, God sent Him out of the deepest of love for all of mankind and to provide grace to the human race, including those who, even at this very hour, do not believe in God or His Son and to those who are too caught up in the world to care about anything spiritual.

> *Like a mother who watches over her child in a sea of children, God looks about this earth at His people. He sees our raw emotions, our struggles, joys, and heartaches.*

Note the little two-letter word "so" in verse 16. "So" is that little extra, that addition to make you realize that what is stated is emphatic and undeniable. The words of the apostle Paul (remember him, the former persecutor of Christians?), recorded in Romans 5:8, seem appropriate: "But God demonstrates His own love toward us, in that while we were still sinners, Christ died for us."

## God's Immense Love

God made the first move. God held out His arms in love long before any of us even acknowledged Him as God. God hates sin, and you and I were once bathed in sin. Sin was as much a characteristic of ours as the color of our eyes or the style of our hair. He hates sin, but He loves you despite who you were and who you are. Paul deeply understood, as should we, that we are all sinners (Rom. 3:23). Paul wrote, "By the grace of God, I am what I am" (1 Cor. 15:10). You are nothing without God, but with God, you are everything!

This is your God and my God. He loves you like no human being has, can, or ever will. He wants nothing in return from you except for you to love Him with "all of your heart, soul, and mind" as there is nothing that you could ever do to repay Him for his extraordinary love and compassion expressed by the gift of His Son. I do not deserve even an ounce of that love, and neither do you. That motivates me!

The fact that God loves me when I know me, my thoughts, my foolish acts, and a host of other issues with which I struggle, motivates me to love Him. You know your skeletons in the closet, your evil thoughts, and your poor decisions. Despite all of your issues, the apostle John wrote in 1 John 4:19, "We love Him because He first loved us."

Those words are so simple yet so powerful and uplifting. Keep them close to your heart and ever on your mind. The love that God showers upon me every day and through offering His Son on the cross motivates me to serve Him to a greater degree now than in the past. I want to show my appreciation for how God has blessed me by obeying and serving Him through building up the faith of my brethren and expanding the borders of His Kingdom by sharing the gospel. I want to minister and serve those around me, since as I do this I am essentially ministering to Christ, who laid down His life for me.

The more I value God's love for me, His sacrifice, and grace, the more motivated I am to serve Almighty God. Yes, we will become discouraged from time to time. That happens; we are human. However, with the right motivation, these times will be minimal in frequency and duration. That is exactly what I'm trying to do to get closer to God each day and minimize Satan's influence on me. Again, the more I value and appreciate the degree of God's love toward me specifically, the more likely I will be to love and serve Him each day.

## CHALLENGE #2: ❖❖❖❖❖❖

Think about this past week. Were there any acts in your life that indicated to God that you love Him? If so, write them down. Also, could any of those acts have been seen by others as evidence of your love for God? If so, again write those down.

# Chapter 3

# Jesus: How It Can Happen

The bonds between family members are often powerful, aren't they? Think about a little six-year-old boy and his eleven-year-old sister. By the way, I was once six years old with an eleven-year-old sister. Now, I was not at all difficult for my sister, so none of what follows is autobiographical (at least according to me). The other party might disagree.

At home, these two kids might fight like a couple of tomcats. The little brother can do no right in the eyes of the sister. He is always into her stuff, taking her toys, tearing them up, and harassing her to play with him when she has "better things to do." Sometimes she wonders why her parents saw the necessity in having him! (Again, I can't fathom my sister thinking of me this way. Surely not!) The big sister often complains to her friends about her little brother and how he is a constant pain in her neck. She goes on and on about him so much that her friends may just be thankful that they don't have to put up with such a menace, but if someone tries to hurt that vermin—excuse me, that little brother of hers—what happens? You would think that he's an angel sent down from heaven, and whoever is attacking him is nothing short of the devil himself. Even one of the big sister's friends suddenly becomes the enemy if she speaks ill of her little brother. She will defend her little brother with ferocity perhaps second only to a mother defending her children.

Why? Because that little, snotty-nosed, six-year-old boy, as silly, annoying, and mean as he may be to her, is *her* brother and is a part of *her* family. She loves him, not because of anything he does for her, but because of their relationship. They are a family. God calls His people a family, with God the Father, Jesus the Son, and us. Second Corinthians 6:18 quotes a prophecy originally from the Old Testament, "I will be a Father to you, and you shall be My sons and daughters, says the LORD Almighty." We are also called sons and daughters, which means that Jesus is our brother! Romans 8:14 says, "For as many as are led by the Spirit of God, these are sons of God."

> *Jesus effectively argues our case before Almighty God as to why God should forgive us and shower us with His grace.*

Let's think about Jesus as our big brother for a moment. The Bible tells us that Jesus faced the same challenges and temptations that we face on a daily basis (Heb. 2:17–18). He has been there. He knows how difficult life can be. He knows what it is to struggle with Satan's temptations. This unique relationship—as an older sibling, if you will—inspires the comforting words found in 1 John 2:1, ". . . And if anyone sins, we have an Advocate with the Father, Jesus Christ the righteous."

Consider that word "Advocate." It is meaningful and powerful. The word gives the idea of a defense attorney (Jesus) standing in a courtroom with His client (you and me) and the Judge (God). Jesus effectively argues our case before Almighty God as to why God should forgive us and shower us with His grace. Imagine the exchange:

> **GOD**: OK, here we have Joe Smith who has been a drunk and frequently uses my name in vain. He also has been negligent in his responsibilities as a husband and father. Joe also has a problem with frequent lying and has on occasion stolen from his employer. He is far from kind and loving to those around him. Joe could have done much more with his life and been far better to his family.
>
> **Jesus**: Father, indeed you are correct about Joe. He has been a drunk and has had a filthy mouth along with being a disappointment as a husband and father. You also noted his lying and stealing issues and his general lack of a loving and kind spirit. I do not deny any of your characteristics of Joe.
>
> However, Joe is your child. He repented, was baptized, and He is a Christian. He struggles with the temptations of the world, and I can relate to how difficult those are. However, Joe is trying. He prays often for forgiveness and strength while enduring temptations, many of which came from poor decisions in his past. He is making an effort to clean up his life, and he is attempting to reconcile his relationship with You, Father, and with those around him on earth. Therefore, based upon my blood that was shed on the cross and your incomparable grace, I ask You to forgive him and restore him in Your sight.
>
> **GOD**: Granted. Joe is clean; his sins are forgotten in my eyes.

Really? Yes, really!

This is an advocate: someone who pleads your case on your behalf in the most effective manner toward the one who is judging you. If you are a Christian, this is what you have in Jesus Christ. Let's take this thought a step further and consider it from a different angle. Remember Genesis 1:26–27 we mentioned in chapter 2 of this book? Here's a reminder: "Let Us make man in Our image, according to Our likeness . . . So God created man in His *own* image; in the image of God He created him." Do you know who the "Us" is? God, Jesus, and the Holy Spirit. That means, along with what we read in John 1:1, that Jesus was with God from the beginning. Therefore, by having Christ as our Advocate, not only do we have someone who pleads our case before God, but in Christ we have someone who knows God in an intimate manner and has known Him since the beginning. So, you have Jesus Christ, the Advocate, who knows the Judge and what satisfies the Judge, and He also knows what makes us do what we do when we are tempted. Who better to go before Almighty God and to argue our case than Jesus?

What makes all this possible is the sacrifice that was made on the cross of Calvary some two thousand years ago. Take a few moments with me and consider that immense sacrifice. Please do not hurry through this next section, as I propose to you that keeping this sacrifice in our hearts and minds on a daily basis is paramount to living everyday Christianity every single day of our lives. Again, slow down for a few moments and meditate on these next several paragraphs.

When Jesus went up that hill called Mount Calvary on that fateful Friday morning, He was exhausted and experiencing pain that you or I cannot possibly fathom. You see, by the time He was to be thrown on the cross later that morning, He had already been beaten to within an eyelash of his life. His back would have been a grizzly sight with parts of his shoulder blades exposed, along with his ribs and most of his back muscles, because with that amount of beating, virtually no skin would have been left.

Add to this the effect that the enormity of His sacrifice was having on His emotions. We can only imagine. What we do know is that it caused Him to plead with His Father on the night before the crucifixion that if there was some other way, some other manner in which the sins of the world could be eliminated that it could be done so He could avoid the cross. That request was not granted.

Here you have a man, the Son of God, the Prince of Peace, who is a mangled and bloody mess, bare of any clothes, already in astonishing pain and anguish, and it's about to get a whole lot worse. Put yourself at the cross. The men throw a bloody Jesus down to the ground on top of two beams of wood, intersecting into a cross. They take his arm, press it against the plank of wood parallel to the ground, grab a huge iron nail, place the point of the nail at the bottom of his hand or wrist, send the hammer crashing down onto the head of that nail, pushing it through the flesh and bone of a man. Not just any man—the Son of God, Jesus the Christ. Blood starts oozing out of one hand. They take the other hand and do the same. Imagine the shock He was experiencing—how with each nail in the hand his back would jerk upward in response to the incredible pain. Again, blood is coming out from the horrible wound in his hand.

Then, the executioners take the feet of Jesus, put them one on top of the other, place the iron nail on the top foot, and slam the hammer onto the nail, driving the nail through both feet and into the cross. Christ surely groans in horror and feels the throb of each heartbeat and the blood rushing through the wounds of His hands and feet.

Next, the cross is lifted up and placed into the ground, with Jesus likely hanging only a short distance from the ground, in almost a teasing manner. It is at this point that the pain shoots up another level, as the strain on his shoulders, back, and legs rises because with each breath he takes, he stretches and tears more flesh near the nails and his back.

There is more. A crown of thorns is placed on His head, and surely it wasn't just laid on top of His head; rather it would have been pushed down upon his head so that the thorns pierced through the thin skin covering his skull. Now look at Him, your Savior. He has blood and sweat rolling down his face, into His eyes, and His body is not even recognizable. For six excruciating hours He hangs on that cross. He has folks come by and spit on Him, hit Him, and ridicule Him. As those six hours tick away, the groans of the Savior become less frequent, and His breaths become shallower, until finally, they end.

The same Jesus who was with God in the beginning, of whom we were made in his likeness, who left the perfection and tranquility of heaven, was now dead. Do you know why? "Well, it was because of these evil men who stuck him on the cross," you might say. Wrong! Jesus could have called a legion of angels and destroyed every single man who contributed to that horrible event. It was because of you and me—our sins. We are the reason that He was shamelessly whipped and then hung on that cross. Yet, He loves us.

As for those folks who were at the scene, whether they were the executioners or mockers, He said of them, in some of His final words, "Father, forgive them, for they do not know what they do." Understand that God loved the men that had killed His Son, along with you and me, more than the well-being of His Son. Don't leave that thought. Think about it. Here it is again. God loved the men, including us, who were responsible for the killing of His Son more than the well-being of His Son. His love for those killing His Son, along with His love for you and me, kept His Son on the cross. No nails could have done that.

That is incredible. We have an awesome God and a loving brother in Jesus Christ.

> *The same Jesus who was with God in the beginning, of whom we were made in his likeness, who left the perfection and tranquility of heaven, was now dead.*

That sacrifice motivates me and brings me to tears right now as I write these words. I weep because of how much He loved me—a man full of weaknesses and subject to sin. Both the Father and the Son love me to this day even though I'm the reason for the suffering of Christ. Look inside yourself; look at your weaknesses; look at all the times you sin and fail God; look at all the instances in which you've failed to be a good mother, father, son, daughter, friend, minister, or teacher. God sees those times, and He and His Son still love you and keep on loving you.

The apostle Paul described the sacrifice of Christ in this way in Romans 8:38–39: "For I am persuaded that neither death nor life, nor angels nor principalities nor powers, nor things present nor things to come, nor height nor depth, nor any other created thing, shall be able to separate us from the love of God which is in Christ Jesus our Lord." What unparalleled, incredible love our God has for us through His Son, our Savior, Jesus Christ!

### CHALLENGE #3: ➤➤➤➤➤➤➤

Read every account of Jesus' death on the cross (Matthew 27–28; Mark 14–15; Luke 22–23; and John 18–19). Perhaps you have never read these eight chapters in succession. While it will take some time, I plead with you to read them, dwell upon them, and let the words and events of the crucifixion penetrate your heart.

## Chapter 4

# So, There's This Family I Know . . .

Remember the song "We Are Family" by Sister Sledge in 1979? That song became the theme song for the 1979 Pittsburgh Pirates, who eventually won the World Series that year. The team used that song to connect with their fans and the players with one another. It essentially produced a "we are all in this together" mentality. Why make such an effort? What benefit came from it? The old saying goes, "There is power in numbers." How true that is! When a collection of individuals is striving for the same goal, they can support one another and rely on one another.

Why do you think there are so many weight-loss groups and alcoholic recovery groups? It's because numbers often equal support. If Mary, Barbara, and Jenny are trying to lose weight together, they motivate one another. (There's that word "motivate" again. See how important it is?) When one does not want to walk on the treadmill, the others can encourage her. When another one of the three wants to eat those powdered doughnuts, someone is there to help her.

This description also fits with God's family. His family includes God, His Son, as well as the Church, which, of course, is comprised of Christians. Therefore, if you are a Christian, you are a part of this glorious and never-ending family. It is a family full of love from God and Jesus down to each Christian. There is no greater family of which you could be a part, and the benefits of being in this family are eternal.

Granted, not all of us grew up in an ideal family, and perhaps your family situation right now is not that great. For you, it might be difficult to comprehend what a loving, do-anything-for-you family is like. Regardless of your earthly family situation, know that you can be a part of the greatest family the world has ever known or will ever know.

## God's Family—How Great It Is!

We touched on this family concept a bit in the last chapter, but let's dig a little deeper and see just how great it is to be a part of God's family. Romans 8:14–17 says,

> For as many as are led by the Spirit of God, these are sons of God. For you did not receive the spirit of bondage again to fear, but you received the Spirit of adoption by whom we cry out, "Abba, Father." The Spirit Himself bears witness with our spirit that we are children of God, and if children, then heirs—heirs of God and joint heirs with Christ, if indeed we suffer with *Him*, that we may also be glorified together.

Paul is writing to the Christians in Rome, and if you are a Christian, Paul is also writing to you as well by the inspiration of God.

Notice the "family" words used in this text. Look at the word "adoption." To be adopted is to be legally moved from one family to another. While you still may have some characteristics of your old family (your voice, movements, etc.), you are now a chosen, full-fledged member of a new family. Other terms in the passage such as "children" and "sons" reiterate the family relationship.

This whole family relationship in the Church is quite beautiful. When you become a Christian, God has adopted you into His family. That family is the Church (Acts 2:40–47), and His Son, Jesus Christ, is Savior of the body, which is the Church (Eph. 2:22–23; 5:23). Stop for a moment and grasp the beauty here. Neither you nor I deserve to be part of such a family. It does not matter who you are, what your status is, how much money you've earned, or how great you have been to your family. We do not deserve it. We are sinners. We are so far away from the love and goodness of God and Christ that we do not deserve to even be a servant in that family. We are like the Prodigal Son, who you may remember reasoned with himself that perhaps he could go back to his father and be a servant. Like the Prodigal Son, we deserve far, far less, but God gives us oh so much more!

> *Like the Prodigal Son, we deserve far, far less, but God gives us oh so much more!*

In Romans 8, we are also called "heirs." What does "heir" mean to you? An heir is someone who inherits something due to the relationship they have with someone else. It is not that they have worked for it; it is not as though they deserved to receive this possession. It's simply because of the relationship. So, what this tells me is that I, as a Christian, have an inheritance. What is the inheritance? It is heaven! Here is how it is described in 1 Peter 1:4, 9: "to an inheritance incorruptible and undefiled and that does not fade away, reserved in heaven for you . . . receiving the end of your faith—the salvation of *your* souls." What I, as a Christian, receive from God is an inheritance that I don't deserve and that will never grow old. It will be as outstanding on Day 1 of heaven (if there will be some type of "day" in heaven) as it will be on Day 1,000,001.

## The Two Things I Must Do

Now, let's look at one more word in this beautiful passage in Romans 8. "Abba," used in verse 15, is a term of endearment, and when combined with "Father" conveys the idea of an extremely loving and personal relationship between Christians and their Father in heaven. We might compare God to the earthly father who not only provides for the physical needs of his children (Matt. 6:25–34) but also seeks a deeper emotional relationship with them (Phil. 4:6–7).

> *He is not, as some might portray Him, the grumpy old man sitting in the sky waiting for humans to slip up. In fact, He couldn't be any further from that.*

We are blessed to have such a deep, intimate relationship with the Creator of the universe, Almighty God in heaven. We have a compassionate and loving Father who is sympathetic to our innermost needs and desires, not to mention our heartaches. He is not, as some might portray Him, the grumpy old man sitting in the sky waiting for humans to slip up. In fact, He couldn't be any further from that.

What about us? Do we have obligations as a member of this glorious family? Yes, we most certainly do. Do you recall when Jesus was asked by the lawyer which was the most important commandment? He said, "You shall love the Lord your God with all your heart, with all your soul, and with all your mind. And *the* second *is* like it: 'You shall love your neighbor as yourself'" (Matt. 22:37, 39). If you have repented of your sins and been baptized, you are a member of the Lord's Church, and consequently, you are a part of this glorious family.

Just like with any family, there are responsibilities of each family member. Obviously, God, the Father, and Jesus, our brother, have done their part. But what do we need to do specifically? Are there things we need to be doing every single day as members of this family? Yes, and these are summed up in the two greatest commandments we just referred to.

The first commandment essentially is to love our Father. What does that mean? Well, our Father tells us, via words from His Son, "If you love Me, keep My commandments" (John 14:15); "He who has My commandments and keeps them, it is he who loves Me" (John 14:21); "He who does not love Me does not keep My words" (John 14:24); "If you keep My commandments, you will abide in My love, just as I have kept my Father's commandments and abide in His love" (John 15:10); and "You are My friends if you do whatever I command you" (John 15:14).

Sounds simple, doesn't it? It also sounds much like the passage in James 1 that you read for Challenge #1. Go back and read that, please. It's James 1:22–25. It is quite simple. Look at all of what God has done for you as well as the sacrifice that His Son made for you. All they ask from you in return is to obey the Word of God. In order to do that we need to read His Word, read it often, put it into practice, and reread it to make sure we do not forget what He has told us. Oh wait! Again, that is exactly what we find in James 1:22–25.

To summarize, as a Christian, you are part of the greatest family the world has ever known. You have the best Father anyone could have. He cares more for you than you can comprehend. You have a big brother in Jesus Christ who took the punishment you deserved from your Father and who still advocates between you and your Father. Finally, you have millions of brothers and sisters on this earth who, while not being earthly blood relatives, are in fact relatives through the blood of Jesus Christ. What a family!

## CHALLENGE #4: ❯❯❯❯❯❯❯

What things do you do or fail to do from day to day or week to week that disappoint God? Consider how you can correct those and be more pleasing to your Father, Almighty God.

# Chapter 5

# You Gotta Love Our Father

Recall some of the concepts from chapter 2. We looked at the idea that the more we value what God has done for us, the more we will be dedicated to living for Him and, I would add, the more we will want to love Him. Love is one of those terms that is sometimes difficult to define. Go ahead and try to think of a good definition. It is even harder to think of a one-word synonym.

What is love? What are expressions or actions that are evidences of love? In the next chapter, we will look at loving one another. For now, the question is this: How do I and how should I love God? After all, God does not need my love. There is not anything I can do to help God. He does not need someone to lean on or talk with, nor does he need someone to "be there" for Him.

You might say, "God has done so much for me. Look at my life. I have a roof over my head, food to eat, a close friend or two. If I sat here for a while, I would no doubt have a long list of what He has done for me. I just feel like I need to do something for Him. I want to love Him and express how thankful I am to Him."

In John 14:2–6, you may recall Jesus said, "In my Father's house are many mansions [rooms, in some translations]" and that He has gone to "prepare a place for you." Jesus is clearly talking about heaven, where I, and hopefully you, are planning to spend eternity. Thomas asks Jesus about the path to get there. Jesus responds in verse 6, "I am the way, the truth, and the life. No one comes to the Father except through Me." You just said you need to do something to show your love and gratitude toward God since He has done so much for you. OK, here is what you need to do. In verse 15 of that same chapter, Jesus said, "If you love Me, keep My commandments." A little later, in verse 21, we read, "He who has My commandments and keeps them, it is he who loves Me." Notice a theme developing?

There are more verses like this. In John 14:23 we read, "If anyone loves Me, he will keep My word; and My Father will love him." John 15:10 says, "If you keep My commandments, you will abide in My love, just as I have kept My Father's commandments and abide in His love." If you were looking for some complex, highly technical answer for how to love God, then I'm sure you are disappointed. However, if you are like me and prefer simplicity, then here you go: keeping the commandments of God equals loving Him. That's it, plain and simple. So many folks try to make it more than what it is. They want to add or subtract things that they don't want to do. If they will just strive to follow the commandments of God, they will be on the right path.

## Following God by Command and Example

Let's dig a little deeper. What are those commandments? Go back to the verse mentioned above, John 15:10, which says, "If you keep My commandments, you will abide in My love, just as I have kept My Father's commandments and abide in His love." Note that Jesus is telling me that He followed God's commandments. Therefore, with some simple reasoning, it is clear that if I follow Jesus, then I am following God.

Again, let's drill a little deeper. We can look to Christ and follow Him both by keeping the commandments He gave us, as well as by following His examples as recorded in the Bible. Let's look at some examples of each.

In the Sermon on the Mount, Jesus said in Matthew 6:14–15, "For if you forgive men their trespasses, your heavenly Father will also forgive you. But if you do not forgive men their trespasses, neither will your Father forgive your trespasses." That's rather clear, though certainly not easy at times. Forgive other people if you expect to be forgiven. Here's another example. Jesus said in Mark 16:16, "He who believes and is baptized will be saved; but he who does not believe will be condemned." In that passage, Jesus is telling His disciples what they are to preach. This is a message directly from Christ. Essentially Jesus is telling his apostles to tell people they need to do this: believe and be baptized so you can be saved. If they do these things, they will be obeying God.

> *Yes, we all have to work for a living, we have families we love, and there are things we like to do, but, at the end of the day, those things will fade away.*

Let's look at one more example. This one is a little less specific, so we will have to dig a little deeper. In the Sermon on the Mount in Matthew 6:19–21, Jesus says, "Do not lay up for yourselves treasures on earth, where moth and rust destroy and where thieves break in and steal; but lay up for yourselves treasures in heaven, where neither moth nor rust destroys and where thieves do not break in and steal. For where your treasure is, there your heart will be also." Again, this is a command. Jesus says for us not to focus on the treasures of earth. Those things cannot be our priority if we are going to love Him. Yes, we all have to work for a living, we have families we love, and there are things we like to do, but, at the end of the day, those things will fade away.

Think about this. Have you ever been to an estate auction? Here's how this usually goes down. An older person has collected some things over the course of a lifetime. (Nothing wrong with that.) Let's say it's a mother with three kids. She passes away. The three kids, often after squabbling over some things, look around and say, "We don't really want any of this stuff. We should just sell it and the house and split the proceeds." Again, nothing wrong with that, but think about this. All the things you collect are likely going to be thrown away or sold by the next generation. Those dishes Grandma Mae had will eventually be accidently broken or thrown away. Even the family pictures that are so precious to you, and understandably so, will one day be lost or thrown away. Even the house that the kids' mom took such good care of is going to be sold to someone else. That person or that family may or may not keep the house in as good care. There's nothing the kids can do about it. Jesus commanded not to fall in love with "treasure" or the things of this earth. These things are going to be destroyed. After all they are perishable.

However, He also commanded us to lay up treasures in heaven. What is He telling me? Jesus is telling me to be focused on heaven and godly things. Consider what Paul said in a passage that directly relates to this idea. In Philippians 4:8, we read, "Finally, bretheren, whatever things *are* true, whatever things *are* noble, whatever things *are* just, whatever things *are* pure, whatever things *are* lovely, whatever things *are* of good report, if *there is* any virtue and if *there is* anything praiseworthy—meditate on these things." Focus on heavenly things that are pure and eternal.

## Learning from Christ's Example

Let's go back to the cross and look at one of the statements Jesus made there. Recall that we looked earlier in this chapter at how Jesus said in the Sermon on the Mount that we were to forgive others. In Luke 23:34, Jesus says, "Father, forgive them, for they do not know what they do." Jesus directly forgave those who were hurting Him while on the cross. We are to do the same, and we can see that both in the commandments of Jesus in the Sermon on the Mount as well as by observing his actions.

Here is another example of observing and following Christ. In the times of Christ, it was common for slaves or servants to wash the feet of guests before they sat down to eat a meal. The guests would sit down at the table, not like we do in a chair, but rather they would be gathered together eating on the floor. In John 13, we see Jesus and His disciples together to eat a meal. The meal has already begun, and nobody has stepped up to wash anyone else's feet. In the eyes of many, the washer signaled that he was inferior to the others. Not surprisingly, none of the disciples stepped up, so Jesus got up and began to wash the disciples' feet to teach them a lesson of servitude. The one person in the room who was superior to the others was the very one who lowered or humbled Himself to do the work of a slave. Jesus then says in John 13:15, "For I have given you an example, that you should do as I have done to you."

> *We are all created by God in His image. Regardless of my lot in life, I must be willing to serve the needs of others as evidenced by the example of Christ.*

What do I learn from this observation of Christ's life? If I am going to be pleasing to God and Jesus, then I need to serve those around me. I ought not to think more highly of myself than those around me. We are all created by God in His image. Regardless of my lot in life, I must be willing to serve the needs of others as evidenced by the example of Christ.

## Love and Obedience—Inseparable

How do you love God? You obey Him. You read about the life of Christ, study His commandments and His life, work to obey those commandments, and emulate how He treated those around Him. Then you study the characteristics of the Church as seen in the book of Acts and, after that in your Bible, the epistles to the churches and individuals. Next, you consider the words found in the final book of Revelation. Recall those words of Paul, as seen in 2 Timothy 3:16: "All Scripture *is* given by inspiration of God, and *is* profitable for doctrine, for reproof, for correction, for instruction in righteousness, that the man of God may be complete, thoroughly equipped for every good work." We have to study the Scriptures because that's where we find out what God has told us to do and not do. Sound familiar? Remember that formula from James 1:22–25?

LOOK + LOOK + DO = SUCCESS

In this case, LOOK + LOOK + DO = OBEDIENCE. Of course, with obedience comes success: eternal success. Jesus illustrated this when He gave the parable of the houses built by the wise man and the foolish man in Matthew 7. The wise man built his house upon the rock, and the foolish man built his house upon the sand. The winds and rain came, and the foolish man's house was destroyed while the wise man's house stood. Why? As you may recall, the description of both men begins with the fact that they heard the teachings of Jesus. However, Jesus says the foolish man did not follow the commandments, while the wise man obeyed those commands.

That story should resonate with us. If I fail to put God first and obey His commands, my life is nothing more than a house built on sand. When the storms of life come, what little faith I have will likely be swept away. However, if I am following the commands of God, regardless of whatever is happening in my life, I am building a house unshakable by Satan and whatever he may throw upon me. That same house will one day be exchanged for that "mansion" Jesus is preparing now for His faithful followers.

### CHALLENGE #5: ▶▶▶▶▶▶▶

Skim through the Gospels and look for interactions Jesus had with those around Him. Study those and consider what attributes He displayed that you also need to have in your life.

# Chapter 6

# You Gotta Love Each Other

Years ago I heard a story about a Christian college professor who was teaching a course on love. The final exam would be given for one group on Tuesday morning at 9:00 a.m. and at noon for the other group. For a change of pace, he stated that the exam would be given in the backyard of his home just a few miles off campus. He even told the students that the only exam topic would be "helping those in need." Each student group was to drive to the professor's home. Tuesday came, and they made it to the professor's house to take the exam on helping those in need.

The next day the professor gathered the students for one last meeting of the class. He asked for some comments regarding the exam. A number of the students indicated that the exam seemed rather difficult. After a few minutes of comments, the professor let them in on a little secret. He asked both groups if they noticed something different on their way to the professor's house, something that stood out on their way to his home. Neither group said anything. Everyone said things looked normal. Nothing was out of the ordinary. The professor further prodded them and asked if they remember seeing the elderly woman trying to carry some heavy plastic grocery bags or the family whose car had broken down just up the street from the professor's home.

One of the students asked the professor, "Wait, how did you know?" Then reality struck. The students had missed the "exam." The professor stated that the exam wasn't really the series of questions they saw on the papers they filled out. The exam was whether they would put into practice what they had been taught during the entire semester.

The professor stated, "Am I disappointed that you didn't help the elderly woman or the family I asked to play the part yesterday? Yes. Even more disappointing, though, and you young people aren't alone in this, you even failed to notice those in need. Remember I asked if you saw anything out of the ordinary. You stated that you had not. What that tells me is that you weren't looking for opportunities to show your love to those around you."

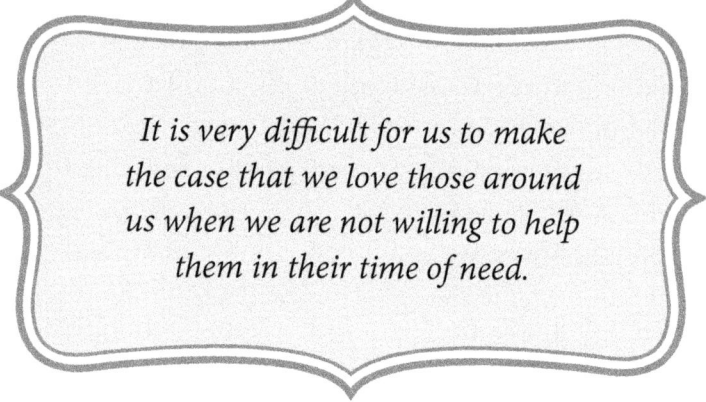

*It is very difficult for us to make the case that we love those around us when we are not willing to help them in their time of need.*

Like the professor said, the students are not alone both in their failure to see those in need as well as their unwillingness to stop and help those in need. We are all guilty of this from time to time. Let me ask you something. What is the evidence that someone loves another individual? Isn't love shown by what people do for others? Look what James said in James 2:15–16: "If a brother or sister is naked and destitute of daily food, and one of you says to them, 'Depart in peace, be warmed and filled,' but you do not give them the things which are needed for the body, what *does it* profit?" James here is talking about the relationship of faith and works, but this certainly relates to faith and love as well. After all, if you were trying to see whether a mother loved her children, would you not look to what she had done for her children? You might see whether she protected her children, encouraged her children, hugged her children, provided for them, and a host of other tangible actions.

The same is true for us. It is very difficult for us to make the case that we love those around us when we are not willing to help them in their time of need. Consider what the apostle John wrote in 1 John 3:18: "My little children, let us not love in word or in tongue, but in deed and in truth." That's similar to what we just looked at from the book of James. But John, by the inspiration of God, did not stop there. He ramped up the necessity of loving those around us. If you have even the slightest inkling of not wanting to love those around you, then meditate on these verses. In 1 John 4:20–21 we read, "If someone says, 'I love God,' and hates his brother, he is a liar; for he who does not love his brother whom he has seen, how can he love God whom he has not seen? And this commandment we have from Him: that he who loves God *must* love his brother also." The way I read that is loving those around us is not optional. It is absolutely, 100 percent a requirement!

## That Great "Love Your Brother" Story

Now, take a look at the first story I think of when I consider the obligation we have to love those around us. It is the story of the Good Samaritan (Luke 10:25–37). You recall that the Samaritan man was the only one of the three men (the others were a priest and a Levite) who helped the man who was robbed. Now the other two knew better. They both saw the man but decided to take a pass on helping him. However, the Samaritan, whose people were despised by the Jews, decided to help. In fact, not only did the Samaritan clean the wounds of the man who was left for dead, he gave the innkeeper two denarii, which may have provided the man with up to twenty-four days to stay at the inn. But the Samaritan wasn't finished! He told the innkeeper that if the care of the man cost more, he would be back and pay him more.

Here is a person who is despised by many of the religious people of the day who actually knew what it was to love his neighbor. He treated him like family, if you will. He gave of his time and his resources to help someone he didn't know and who, given that he was just robbed, probably would never be able to repay him.

Now, don't get me wrong, I know we live in an age in which there are con artists galore and all types of scams. If you or I helped every person that asked for help, we would be broke. However, there are plenty of opportunities to show your love toward others. We must understand that loving our neighbor isn't a suggestion that God gave us; it is a command. Remember in Matthew 22:37–39 that when Jesus was asked by the lawyers what were the greatest commands, Jesus said, "'You shall love the LORD your God with all your heart, with all your soul, and with all your mind.' This is *the* first and great commandment. And *the* second *is* like it. 'You shall love your neighbor as yourself.'" Note Jesus did not say that we *should* love; He said, "*shall* love."

## A Little Self-Evaluation

So, let's think about that concept and evaluate ourselves.

1. Do you love the people around you?
2. Do you love those with whom you attend church services?
3. Do you love those who aren't necessarily loving toward you?

Hopefully, you answered yes to all of those. If you did not, or if maybe you had to struggle to say "yes," let me share some thoughts with you. Just like me, you are not perfect either. Like me, you have said things that hurt feelings, and you've done things or failed to do things you should have done, and consequently, you have hurt people. You have made mistakes in your life, perhaps the same as those who are in need around you, yet you were fortunate enough to escape the consequences they face. That person may have done everything right in their life, but because of a company going out of business, a drunk driver, or a terrible disease, they are hurting.

The fact is if we are not willing to love everyone around us, then we are failing God. Remember, Jesus said this is the second greatest commandment, and the apostle John wrote that we cannot claim to love God if we don't love others. Please consider the following: yes, we need to major in loving God, but we need to minor in loving those around us. In Galatians 6:10, Paul said, "Therefore, as we have opportunity, let us do good to all, especially to those who are of the household of faith."

The people around you who need help aren't any lesser people than you are. Just like you, they were created "in the image of God." The situation they are in now may or may not be due to choices they've made, but regardless of whether they initiated their problems, they are still loved by God and His Son, and they should be loved by those around them.

## Why Loving Others Isn't Optional

Let me give you some more encouragement to love others. We saw that the apostle John wrote that we must love others. If we are going to claim to love God, then we must not love with our words only. We also read what Paul said about helping all, especially the brethren. There are plenty of verses speaking to God's commands for us to love one another. There is also a rather ominous warning. If everything else you have read in this chapter has not convinced you of the necessity of loving others, then I have one more passage for you.

In Matthew 25, we find a window into Judgment Day. This chapter includes the parable of the talents (we will consider that in the next chapter), but it closes with a look at the time in which people will be separated.

Please put this book down for a moment and read Matthew 25:31–46 in your own Bible. Then come back.

Powerful, isn't it? I want you to see something here. While I believe doctrine is extremely important, the issue discussed here regarding Judgment Day is whether people loved those around them. Both the righteous and the unrighteous question Jesus and say that they never saw him hungry, thirsty, a stranger, naked, or in prison. I think if every single person reading this book—and its author—were we to see Jesus thirsty, they would give Him a glass of water. Why, we would probably give Him glass after glass of water! And, if Jesus was hungry, I imagine we would open our kitchen to Him, offer Him anything and everything we had, and take Him to the local restaurant. We would even offer Him food to go too. And, if Jesus was without a home, we would open our doors for Him, pay for His hotel, or do whatever He needed. And, if Jesus was in prison, we would certainly visit Him.

> *While I believe doctrine is extremely important, the issue discussed here regarding Judgment Day is whether people loved those around them.*

When was the last time we did any of these things for those around us? How often have we turned a blind eye to those around us? Let me be the first to say, "GUILTY." But, if I am going to have everyday Christianity every single day, then I need to open my eyes to the needs of others and address those needs. (More on that in chapter 8.) It isn't enough to wish these people well or to just pray for them. If God has given us the means to help those around us, we need to do just that. Again, we cannot possibly help every person, but we can certainly get involved in the lives of those around us and help them, especially those with whom we worship. How can I sit in the same church building as someone else who has nothing, claim to love them, and not be willing to sacrifice from my own abundance to help them?

Based on all that's been written here, where do you stand? I know for me, as I sit in my house writing this, that I can do far more. Perhaps you are in the same boat. Perhaps, like me, you need to open your eyes and see the opportunities you have to love those around you by getting involved in their lives.

### CHALLENGE #6: ◆◆◆◆◆◆◆

This one may be tough depending on your personality. Send a handwritten note to someone you care about. Tell that person that you love him or her and insist that that individual allow you to help them if there is anything at all you can do. Just imagine how much closer our relationships would be, how much closer our church members would be, if we all did this.

# Chapter 7

# The Quality You Must Have

In the last two chapters, we have discussed the need to love God and those around us. There is no question that in order to please God, we need to love Him by obeying His commandments, and we cannot claim to love God if we are not willing to love those around us. Everyday Christianity requires us to love God every day and to love those around us every day. All that said, there is a quality that we must have in order to live for God. Let's see if you can guess what that is as we go along.

To obey someone, whether a parent, teacher, employer, or the government, requires us to put aside what we may want to do if it conflicts with the one in authority. That was a tough lesson for us to learn when we were youngsters, wasn't it? You may remember when you were young how you wanted to play outside or watch television. However, your mother or father did not agree. Instead, you were told that you needed to do your homework. "Not interested," you thought. Perhaps you thought about reasoning with your parents by using a host of excuses or arguments, but in the end you knew your desire, your will, did not take priority in your house. Eventually, you realized the wisdom in doing your homework.

Now, why did you choose the path of doing your homework? At some point, you humbled yourself before your parents and did not do what you wanted, but you did what they wanted. The quality needed in order to practice everyday Christianity every single day is humility.

## Humility

My favorite biblical story about humility is found in Luke 18:9–14. It is the parable of the Pharisee and the tax collector. Go ahead and read the story in your Bible.

> *If you are arrogant, that arrogance can, and I would dare say often does, lead to thinking less of those around you.*

Sometimes when we read this story, we overlook the very first verse. Recall what is written in verse 9: "Also He spoke this parable to some who trusted in themselves that they were righteous, and despised others."

Did you get that? He was teaching people who were self-righteous and despised others, because despising others is a product of self-righteousness. If you are arrogant, that arrogance can, and I would dare say often does, lead to thinking less of those around you.

Notice that when the Pharisee prayed, he essentially said, "God, congratulations in making me. I mean, you clearly threw away the mold when you made me. There is no person on this earth as pure as the driven snow as I am. Imagine if everyone were like me (yeah, imagine that) and were as good as me." I did embellish there a bit, but that is how

I imagine the mind of this Pharisee. In addition, the Pharisee made sure those around him saw that he was praying. He was all about making sure that everyone knew how great he was.

Contrast Mr. Pharisee with the other man, a tax collector. Remember that tax collectors were rather despised, to put it mildly, back in the days of Jesus. Many of them were cheats. If there was a list of most dishonest professions, I suspect that tax collector would be near or at the top. Unlike the Pharisee, the tax collector's prayer was not elaborate and did not have a "look at how great I am" sense to it. Instead, the only words he said were, "God, be merciful to me a sinner!" Nothing fancy there, just the truth. Jesus wraps up the teaching by stating that the tax collector went down to his house justified. He then went on to say, "for everyone who exalts himself will be humbled, and he who humbles himself will be exalted."

Let's go back to the equation we first considered in chapter 1, which was based on James 1:25.

LOOK + LOOK + DO = SUCCESS

You see, the first LOOK and even the second LOOK aren't too difficult. It is the DO part that is hard. In the next chapter, we'll talk specifics about what we can do. However, for now, let me submit to you that the bridge between knowing what to do and actually doing it is humility. Let me say that again. The bridge between knowing what to do and actually doing what is commanded is the attribute of humility. Humility is what allows our will to be bent into or grafted into God's will. It reminds us of what Paul wrote in Galatians 2:20: "I have been crucified with Christ; it is no longer I who live, but Christ lives in me." Paul also said of Christians, in Romans 12:3, "not to think *of himself* more highly than he ought to think..."

Humility is obviously an attribute we can choose to have or not have. We can be like the Pharisee and be absent of humility, or we can be like the tax collector and be bathed in humility. The apostle Paul was a man of humility. Here is someone who could have been arrogant. In 2 Corinthians 11:22–31, Paul speaks of the life he had endured as an evangelist for Christ. He could have termed himself "Chief Evangelist." He did so much for the cause of Christ. If anyone could be exempt from needing to be humble, we might argue it was Paul.

Yet, humility personified Paul. Recall his words from 1 Corinthians 15:10: "But by the grace of God I am what I am . . . yet not I, but the grace of God *which* was with me." That's humility. As to his highly educated upbringing, and his status prior to becoming a Christian, Paul wrote in Philippians 3:7: "But what things were gain to me, these I have counted loss for Christ."

## Increasing Your Humility

You might say, "Well I understand that humility is vital in serving God, and I would concur that humility is a bridge from knowing what to do and actual obedience. However, how do I become more humble?"

I'm glad you asked. Certainly, a deep and sincere appreciation for what God has done for you is where to start. Keeping the sacrifice of Christ in your heart often—every day, in fact—provides a strong foundation for increased humility. In addition, let me propose to you that if you want more humility, spend much more time in prayer to the Almighty. Let me give you a personal example. Several months ago, I was driving in my car and I turned on the religious station. I recall the speaker talking about the need to pray more often. Soon thereafter, I turned the radio off and thought deeply about that idea. The speaker challenged his listeners to spend thirty minutes a day in prayer. I thought that was a great idea, but I also thought there was something more.

As I grappled with this idea I committed to not only pray that long, but to pray in at least five-minute increments. It changed my life! Why? Because when you pray for that long at one time, you dive deeper into subjects than you do with a quick prayer. I found myself bringing more to God, both in quantity and quality. I prayed more intently for my marriage and for my children than I ever had before. I prayed for my relationships with others in a greater way. As I prayed, I looked more intently at myself, seeing far more clearly the "beam in my own eyes." I asked God for more of His wisdom than I had probably done collectively over my lifetime.

Prayer moved from being something I did before I went to bed and occasionally during the day to a powerful time of the day in which I brought it all before God. I got to the point where I finally just said to God, "I don't know what to do. Please just take over the major decisions of my life, and show me what you want me to do to serve you. Make the choices so blatantly obvious that I can't miss them. Please just push me the way I should go."

Paul told the Christians in Philippians 4:6–7, "Be anxious for nothing, but in everything by prayer and supplication, with thanksgiving, let your requests be made known to God; and the peace of God, which surpasses all understanding, will guard your hearts and minds through Christ Jesus." Are you doing that? Honestly, are you? Notice Paul didn't say, "Pray to God about the big stuff of life." No! Instead he wrote by the inspiration of God to bring everything to God in prayer. I believe everything means everything. God wants to hear from you about anything that concerns you, anything that is troubling you, and anything that is on your mind. God stands ready to hear those prayers.

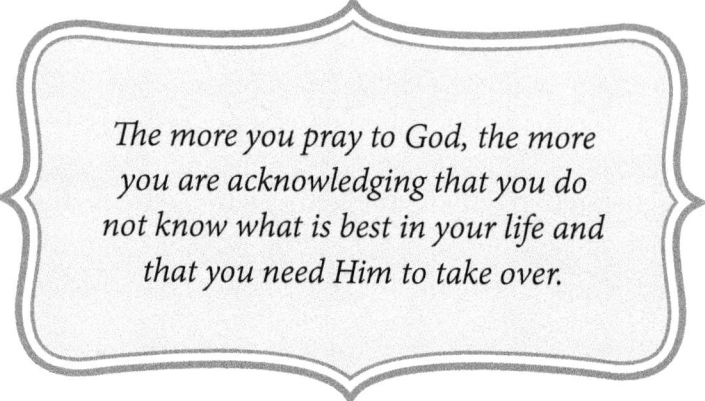

*The more you pray to God, the more you are acknowledging that you do not know what is best in your life and that you need Him to take over.*

You see, the more you spend time praying to God in a deeper way, the more your will becomes grafted into His will. The more you pray to God, the more you are acknowledging that you do not know what is best in your life and that you need Him to take over. You need Him to not only guide you but sustain you, and you are completely dependent on Him. When we do that, we become increasingly obedient to Him. We move from simply knowing what to do from God's Word to actually doing what He says. That's powerful. That's how you get to being an everyday Christian every single day that you walk the face of this earth. You humble yourself under the mighty hand of God the Father.

## The Ultimate Example of Humility

Let me share with you one more story regarding humility. It occurred about two thousand years ago in a garden, and it involved none other than my Lord and Savior, Jesus Christ. Jesus was set to be crucified only hours from the time He was in the garden. The Scripture in Matthew 26:37 says, "... He began to be sorrowful and deeply distressed."

It was the human nature of Christ. As much as He loved you and me, the reality that He was about to endure the most painful method of execution was on his mind. He was going to be the complete sacrifice for your sins and mine (1 John 4:2). Over the next several verses, Jesus asks His Father if there was some other way. Perhaps something different can be done rather than being nailed to a cross, having a crown of thorns thrust on His head, and His side pierced. Yet, in those prayers to the Father, humility flowed from the Savior. Each time he stated to His Father, "Your will be done."

For Jesus, the will of His Father trumped anything He wanted, even the absence of pain via the crucifixion. Notice that the humility of Christ came via his prayer to the Father. For Christ to go through with the crucifixion, something that would run contrary to His will, He had to devote Himself to prayer, and so must we. If we are going to live a life that bends to the will of the Father, we need to be in constant communication with him in prayer. We need to bring anything and everything before the Creator. He is listening. He wants to hear from His children. First Peter 3:12 tells us, "For the eyes of the Lord *are* on the righteous, and His ears are *open* to their prayers." Don't neglect the incredible privilege you have to speak to the one who spoke the universe into existence and knew you even from the womb. Commit yourself to engaging in deeper prayers to God. Humble yourself under His mighty hand.

**CHALLENGE #7:** ◆◆◆◆◆◆◆

Try to pray for at least thirty minutes a day in increments of at least five minutes. Find the time. Pray on your commute to work, pray when you first wake up or lie down to sleep, pray when you're waiting for someone, pray at lunch. Just pray, pray, and pray some more. You will see a difference in your attitude toward God and your perspective on allowing Him to guide your life.

# Chapter 8

# What Can I Do?

A minister was hired to serve a small-town congregation. When he arrived, attendance generally ran around 100. For a few years, the preacher ministered to the people, and he preached sermon after sermon. He was well-liked by the membership and the community. Unfortunately, over those few years, attendance dropped, and the once vibrant programs that the church engaged in were either non-existent or awfully close. While the minister was frustrated, so were the members. The members complained that the church wasn't what it used to be. Conversations were often heard such as, "Our church used to this and that, and we used to be so close as church members." The minister agreed, so he did something rather dramatic.

The little town had a weekly newspaper that was published on Thursdays. So, the minister decided to take out a full-page ad in the paper. However, it was not an ad inviting the people of the small town to an ordinary service. Instead, his full-page ad read, "Come to the funeral service of the Anytown Church at 10:00 a.m. Sunday. We invite everyone and certainly our current members and those who used to attend here." As you might expect, it did not take long that Thursday for the conversation to begin at the local diner, the school, and throughout town. Oh, and the phone rang constantly that morning at the church building.

Sunday came, and the building was packed with nearly 200 people in attendance. The minister had a casket behind him. After finishing the eulogy for the church, he said, "Now, I would ask that those of you who are members here to pass by the casket after the conclusion of our services, as well as those who once attended. While you go up to the casket and pay your respects, look deep inside of the casket, and you will see why this church has died." The people did just that. As they passed by the casket and looked inside, they saw themselves, for the minister had put a mirror inside to show that the people who comprised the church were the reason it had died. If we are not working for the Lord, and we have the talents to do something, we are failing in our obligations.

> *You cannot earn your salvation. You could feed and clothe the world, and it still would not be enough.*

## His Workmanship

Ephesians 2:8–10 says, "For by grace you have been saved through faith, and that not of yourselves; *it is* the gift of God, not of works, lest anyone should boast. For we are His workmanship, created in Christ Jesus for good works, which God prepared beforehand that we should walk in them." The motivation for good works is found in verses 8–9. Paul is telling us that the only reason we are saved is the grace of the Almighty. Get that point, please! You cannot earn your salvation. You could feed and clothe the world, and it still would not be enough. But, you see, that is where so many stop and say, "Well, there you go. Works are not important." No! That's not the point. Again, Paul is telling us that we cannot do enough works to be saved, only God's grace saves us. It's therefore because of God's grace and His abundant love that we should work for Him.

Verse 10 says we are "His workmanship." The idea is that we are finely crafted tools that God has "created for good works." That is your purpose! Please see that! When you became a Christian, you were created to do something, so use your talents. Look in your own Bible at Titus 2:11–14. What did you see in verse 14? The description of Christians here is "zealous for good works." That word in the original Greek conveys the idea of boiling over with passion or being deeply committed." Deeply committed to what? Good works!

Let me say this with all love but also frankness. It is beyond my comprehension how anyone can read through the New Testament or even just the Gospels and somehow reason that he or she does not have an obligation, a requirement, to use his or her talents for God. If I am going to be an everyday Christian every single day, then I need to use what God has given me.

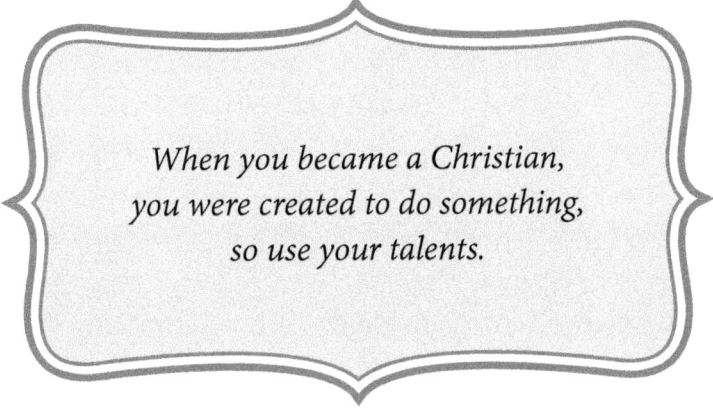

*When you became a Christian, you were created to do something, so use your talents.*

## Using our Talents

We saw in in Matthew 25 a glimpse into Judgment Day and how the two groups were separated by what they had done or had failed to do on behalf of those around them. However, prior to that passage, there is another detailed passage in which Jesus tells us in a parable that we have to use our talents and abilities. It is the parable of the talents. Recall that the one-talent man hid his talent, while the two- and five-talent servants did something with their talents and actually gained more talents. Jesus had some harsh words for the one-talent man. He said, in Matthew 25:30, "And cast the unprofitable servant into the outer darkness. There will be weeping and gnashing of teeth."

We can try to sugarcoat this, but the language of Christ here is quite stern. If we are going to be an everyday Christian every single day, it is imperative that we consider the whole counsel of God (Acts 20:27). God motivates us in a positive manner to work for Him, such as in Ephesians 2, but also in a negative manner, as in Matthew 25. I believe many today measure their commitment to God and serving Him with the punch-card methodology. Now, some of you are too young to know what a punch card is or was. If so, here is a quick history lesson. Punch cards used to be the method by which hourly workers at a business kept track of their time. They would take a thin piece of cardboard, slide it through a slot just below a clock, and the card would be "punched" with the time in which it was placed on the slot. At the end of the week, the time was totaled, and the employee received his or her wages based on the time worked.

In a spiritual sense, here's how this mentality works. Let's say the church you attend has 156 services during the year (Sunday morning, Sunday evening, and Wednesday evening). This type of thinking says,

"Well, I punched in for 141 services this year. That's about a 90 percent clip. That's better than most and would be a letter grade of A in some schools, so I'm good to go with God." To put it another way, my level of dedication to God is measured by how many church services I attend. Look, don't get me wrong, being at these services is important (Hebrews 10:25), but filling a pew as often as the doors are open does not constitute faithfulness.

Look in your Bible. How many examples and commands do you find regarding things we should and should not do versus what should happen when the saints gather together? There's a whole lot more in my Bible on the former rather than the latter. There is something I believe is rather problematic in the Lord's Church related to this necessity of working for the Lord. You see, I have come to observe that we have an agency problem. An agent is someone who does something for someone else: acting on their behalf. Take the sports agent, for example. He or she represents a particular athlete in the negotiation of his playing contract or endorsement contract or a host of other obligations. Again, an agent acts on behalf of someone else or even multiple people.

We buy into the same idea in the church. A few years ago, I came across this ad for a minister.

> A church of around 250 members seeks a full-time minister, with an advanced biblical degree highly preferred. The minister will preach during both services on Sunday and is expected to teach a Bible class on Sunday morning and Wednesday night. In addition to his preaching and teaching duties, the minister should regularly visit the sick of the congregation and those in nursing homes. The minister will also provide counseling as needed to members. Also, the minister will

head the education program, develop and select curriculum, and assign teachers for all classes. The minister should also be prepared to take an active role in the community and represent the church therein.

I'm not exaggerating . . . that's pretty close to what I read. That illustrates the agency problem that I believe is increasingly prevalent in our churches. Pay the preacher and have him and his wife do all the work. Where are the rest of the members? Why aren't they using their talents?

Look at Romans 12:6, "Having then gifts differing according to the grace that is given to us, *let us use them* . . ." Paul then goes on to list a host of talents and abilities God granted to the people there in the early church. Note I said "people," not just the preacher or the deacons. In the same chapter, verse 11, we find these words, "not lagging in diligence, fervent in spirit, serving the Lord . . ." Remember also that the book of Romans was written to all the Christians in Rome, not just those in authority at the local church. All of us have an obligation to use our talents and abilities on behalf of Almighty God!

## Christian Workers—Hang in There

Now, let's end this chapter on a high note. This same Paul also wrote of working for the Lord in 1 Corinthians 15:58, "Therefore, my beloved brethren, be steadfast, immovable, always abounding in the work of the Lord, knowing that your labor is not in vain in the Lord." In other words, "Don't quit; keep working. There's a reward waiting for you." The Hebrew writer put it this way in Hebrews 6:10, "For God *is* not unjust to forget your work and labor of love which you have shown toward His name, *in that* you have ministered to the saints, and do minister." Again, just like Romans, Hebrews is written to Christians—all of us. God does not forget what you do on behalf of Him and those around you. God has not forgotten the hours you spent preparing for the Vacation Bible School class you taught last year. God has not forgotten about the afternoon you gave up to spend with some of the saints who are now in a nursing home. God has not forgotten about the hours you spent working the clothing drive to help clothe the less fortunate in your community. God has not forgotten about the hundreds of cards you have written over the years to those who were ill. God has not forgotten about the time you spent trying to mentor that young girl who was so close to drifting away. God has not forgotten anything you have ever done for Him, your brothers and sisters in Christ, or even those around you. Like Paul said, "your labor is not in vain."

Everyday Christianity, by definition, means more than just showing up for services. It demands serving the Lord and others the remainder of the week.

### CHALLENGE #8: ▶▶▶▶▶▶▶

Get involved. Talk to your elders, deacons, or minister and say, "It's time for me to get off this seat or pew and do something to strengthen and advance the kingdom." Of course, it doesn't have to be through your home church. Go volunteer, help those in need, and, as you have opportunity, tell people why you're doing it.

# Chapter 9

# So, You're a Billboard

Imagine you are headed to a tourist destination. The one that comes to mind for me is Branson, Missouri. In case you are not familiar with Branson, the town has a lot of comedy and country music shows and a host of shops and entertainment. There is plenty to do in Branson.

Of course, being a tourist destination, there is competition for paying customers. So, as I travel west from St. Louis down to Springfield, and then south to Branson, I start to see more and more billboards the closer I get to Branson. I mean billboards galore. They are everywhere on both sides of the road, billboard after billboard after billboard. Why are there so many? Because the billboard is one way the owners of the show promote the show. They want people to know about their show and why they should make sure to see that show while they are in Branson.

If you are a Christian every single day of your life, you are a billboard for Christianity. You may not think about it. In fact, you may not even like it sometimes, but the only Christianity, the only Jesus, the only Bible many people see is you. Every day your actions, your moods, and your words advertise Christianity. You do not have to be a marketing genius to know that the more a billboard stands out from the other billboards, the value of whatever is being advertised goes up.

God tells us that we have to be different from those around us. Paul begins his first letter to the Corinthians by describing the Christians there as "sanctified in Christ Jesus." What does it mean to be sanctified? Well, the Greek word transliterated is *hagizo*, which means "to separate from profane things." Does that describe you? In an ever more profane world, rampant with the practice and promotion of sin everywhere, it is perhaps easier than ever to stand out. I don't mean it is easy to practice being "separate from profane things," but if you are, you certainly stand out in the world today.

Let's say you were put on trial for being a Christian. Would there be enough evidence from your day-to-day lifestyle to convict you? Take your tongue, for example. James warns us of the tongue in James 3:5, when he writes, "Even so the tongue is a little member and boasts great things. See how great a forest a little fire kindles." What words do you use on a daily basis? Is your language different from those around you? Look, if you don't swear or use profane language, you will stand out nearly everywhere anymore. Do you encourage and speak kindly to others, or are you like everyone else around you? Do you choose not to participate in the jokes or profane talk at the water cooler, or do you just join in? Do you engage in gossip and live for the next juicy tidbit you might learn about a coworker, friend, or fellow member of the church you attend? Take a little break and assess yourself. What did you find

> *Let's say you were put on trial for being a Christian. Would there be enough evidence from your day-to-day lifestyle to convict you?*

out? Do you stand out among those around you by what you say as well as what you don't say?

## A Living Sacrifice

Let's look at this idea of sanctification or holiness some more. In Romans 12:1–2, Paul writes,

> I beseech you therefore, brethren, by the mercies of God, that you present your bodies a living sacrifice, holy, acceptable to God, *which is* your reasonable service. And do not be conformed to this world, but be transformed by the renewing of your mind, that you may prove what *is* that good and acceptable and perfect will of God.

How do we maintain our sanctification or holiness? By being "transformed by the renewing of your mind."

We have to do that on a daily basis through prayer and Bible study. We have got plenty of stuff that infiltrates our mind on a daily basis through multiple channels of media and those around us. Try as we might, we cannot escape it. Because of that trap, we need something to counter all the ungodly stuff. Think of it this way: Suppose you had two pitchers, one full of tea and the other full of water. Now, you begin pouring the tea in the glass. Obviously, at that point all you have is tea in the glass. However, then you start to pour the water at the same time. What happens? The tea is watered down. Suppose you begin to pour the water into the glass at a far greater rate than the tea. What happens? There becomes less and less tea and more and more water such that the glass becomes almost entirely water.

That concept is the same with what we put into our mind. The more we put godly things into our mind, the more we push out the sinful thoughts. We looked at this verse earlier, but it bears reference again here. Paul wrote, in Philippians 4:8, "Finally, brethren, whatever things are true, whatever things *are* noble, whatever things *are* just, whatever things *are* pure, whatever things *are* lovely, whatever things *are* of good report, if *there is* any virtue and if *there is* anything praiseworthy—meditate on these things." Meditate; let the encouragement and inspiration you find within God's Holy Word travel within your mind. Think about the crucifixion and resurrection. Think about the promise of heaven. Think about how much God loves you and how much He has blessed you. Meditate upon these and other godly things and transform your mind, which will then transform your actions, your words, and your habits so that indeed you are sanctified and stand out among others.

But why stand out? Because, as was said earlier, you and I need to show the rest of the world what they are missing. Do you know how many people in this world do not have the "peace that passes understanding"? How many people lay awake at night and think about what happens when they die or whether there is more to life than the money, fame, or whatever they are engulfed in?

## Light of Christianity

Few people are going to pick up a Bible and read about Jesus, decide to commit themselves to Him, be baptized, and live the rest of their lives for Christ. They have to see something in us day after day—every day, if you will—that is appealing to them. Like the successful billboard, we have to stand out among all the other billboards competing for their attention.

Consider what Jesus said in Matthew 5:14–16: "You are the light of the world. A city that is set on a hill cannot be hidden. Nor do they light a lamp and put it under a basket, but on a lampstand, and it gives light to all *who are* in the house. Let your light so shine before men, that they may see your good works and glorify your Father in heaven." If you are a Christian, you are a light in this old sinful world. What type of light do you put out? Is it a mere spark seen on occasion when conditions are right? Or is it a white-hot fire that burns passionately for the cause of Christ? Jesus says that your fire should burn so brightly that others can say, "What a bright light she is! Wonder why." Ultimately, the reason for making sure our lights are bright is so others might be drawn to our light and eventually to Almighty God.

Remember our reference earlier to Romans 12:1–2, where Paul talked about the renewing of your mind and being transformed? Let's suppose you do that. What are the attributes that are then produced that make you stand out among those around you? Those attributes are also found in Romans 12:9–21. Go ahead and read those in your own Bible and then come back and continue reading. Think about all those different characteristics found in verses 9–21. They are so very different than what you see around you!

Paul mentioned to "abhor what is evil." We are told today to tolerate evil. He said to "give preference to one another." We are told to climb over whoever you have to in order to get what you want. Paul said to "bless those who persecute you." We are told to not only insult that person but to hurt them more than they hurt you. The list goes on. Can you imagine how much we can stand out and be a walking billboard for

Christ if we can just put on the characteristics seen in those verses? It will be incredible how much we can stand out.

> *The whole idea of standing out in the crowd is so you can tell people about Christ. You see, Peter wasn't talking to another preacher, or some elders, or youth minister.*

You may say, "OK, but what do I do once I stand out?" Peter addressed just this question—and it's a great question. Now remember earlier that we talked about being sanctified and that we as Christians are to be sanctified. First Peter 3:15 says, "But sanctify the Lord God in your hearts, and always *be* ready to *give* a defense to everyone who asks you a reason for the hope that is in you . . ." The whole idea of standing out in the crowd is so you can tell people about Christ. You see, Peter wasn't talking to another preacher, or some elders, or youth minister. No, he was talking to Christians just like you and me. He told them to be ready to tell people about the joy they have in Christ, about the hope that they have for an eternal reward in heaven. The people we tell can dismiss what we say or they can eventually come to Christ; that is their call. All we can do is present the message to them.

## Put Jesus in the Conversation

We need to look every day for opportunities to tell others about Christ or to invite them to our services or just open up some dialogue regarding religion. I am just as guilty as the next person in failing to do this. In fact, let me tell on myself a bit. Just recently, I found myself talking with a twentysomething person with whom I did some business. He seems to be a nice guy, though I don't know him that well. So, I just invited him to our annual Friends and Family Day at my home church. He declined, but as soon as I asked him, I asked myself, "Chad, when was the last time you actually opened your mouth and invited someone to church services?"

Too long, I can tell you that. I became a bit ashamed, to be honest. Here I walk from day to day genuinely in love with God and so grateful for everything He has done for me spiritually and the untold amount of physical blessings He's given me, and yet I failed to tell others. It was a slap in the face. You no doubt have a host of people you see from time to time. If you're trying to be an everyday Christian every day, I am sure you stand out to some degree from at least some of them. Try to say a word for Christ to them, maybe invite them to church services, or have them over to your home and have a few others from church join you. Remember, you are a billboard for Christ. Chances are there are some folks who would love to know why you have so much joy in your heart. Tell them why!

**CHALLENGE #9:** ♦♦♦♦♦♦♦

This one's tough, but it actually accomplishes two goals. Go up to someone you know and see regularly who is not a Christian and ask them how they see you. What do they see in you? You're opening yourself up for them to both praise you and criticize you. After you've done this, invite them to something church-related. You may be surprised to hear the positive response.

## Chapter 10

# It's Not If You Fail but When You Fail

When I'm talking about spiritual failure, it really boils down to sinning against God. What we might term "major mistakes" are things like what David did with Bathsheba and Uriah. What we might term "minor mistakes" are things like the priest and the Levite in the parable of the Good Samaritan. Both are sin. One really is not any different than the other as far as failing in the eyes of God. The reality of sin in our lives, even the Christian's life, is found in Romans 3:23, "for all have sinned and fall short of the glory of God..." Try as you may, you will not be able to completely avoid sin. We do things we should not and fail to do things we should.

What does it mean to sin? Literally, the term means to "miss the mark." Think about it in terms of playing darts. In some versions of darts, you start with a score of 301 or 501, and the object is to eventually get your score to exactly zero. So, you and your opponent each throw three darts with each turn. During the countdown you can reduce your score by hitting anywhere on the dartboard. But, eventually you will be left with a specific number. You may have to keep throwing until you're able to finally put that dart in the mark where it needs to go. Unless you throw that dart in the section corresponding to that specific number, you've missed the mark.

Continually missing the mark in darts can be frustrating. You are so close to winning, to getting things right. Yet, you fail time after time. Anybody else other than me felt the same way regarding sins in their life? You look at yourself and become increasingly frustrated that you keep messing up. Maybe it is a particular sin or maybe it is a hodgepodge of sin. Maybe they are sins of commission or sins of omission. They both count. It is frustrating, isn't it?

## The Chapter Before the Encouraging Chapter

One of my favorite chapters in the Bible is Romans 8. I have read that chapter and reread it. From the first verse, which speaks of the absence of condemnation for the Christian, to the last verse, which talks about nothing being able to separate us from the love of Jesus, it is an encouraging and uplifting chapter. Now, I had read chapter 7 before as well, but, wow! Chapter 8! It doesn't get any more encouraging than that. The apostle Paul, who by inspiration of God penned the words of chapter 8, also wrote the words of chapter 7. Take a couple of minutes and read chapter 7.

Now, aside from Jesus, you might think that Paul did not struggle with sin. Here was someone who had been shipwrecked, beaten, and left for dead. He was persecuted mightily for his dedication to God. Anybody who had that much faith and that much perseverance surely did not have a problem with sin. Wrong! In Romans 7:15, Paul wrote these words, speaking of his sin problem, "For what I am doing, I do not understand. For what I will to do, that I do not practice; but what I hate, that I do." *Ding, ding, ding* . . . does that ring a bell with anyone? Have you felt that you could have written those exact words?

What about Romans 7:19? Consider if you've ever felt this way: "For the good that I will *to do*, I do not do; but the evil I will not *to do*, that I practice." You might say, "Paul, that describes me." Here is quite possibly the greatest evangelist the world has ever known, who gave up everything he had in order to follow Christ, yet he still struggled with sin. How comforting that should be to us! We are not alone. Remember in chapter 1 of this book when I mentioned how we might look around and see so many around us who seem to be living perfect lives, free of any problems. Guess what, they aren't. They just hide them well.

> *Even the apostle Paul struggled with sin, so it should not shock me if from time to time I struggle with sin.*

Please get this. You are not alone in struggling with sin. That does not make you a bad person. That does not make you a failure in the eyes of God. Just because you struggle with sin does not make you any lesser of a Christian or any less precious in the sight of God. Consider what Paul wrote in Romans 7:25, the last verse in the chapter, "So then, with the mind I myself serve the law of God, but with the flesh the law of sin." You may say, "Chad, how does that help me?" Ah, look at the very next words you find that open up Romans 8: "There is therefore now no condemnation to those who are in Christ Jesus, who do not walk according to the flesh, but according to the Spirit." Hallelujah! Praise God! What joy that brings to my soul.

Here is my takeaway from the end of Romans 7 and the beginning of chapter 8. Even the apostle Paul struggled with sin, so it should not shock me if from time to time I struggle with sin. That does not make it right, but it also does not make me a failure. That is, unless you are prepared to say the apostle Paul was a failure. Nope, I didn't think so.

## Looking Above

Here's the problem we sometimes have trying to live as an everyday Christian every single day. We look to ourselves. Woe is me. I've done this, and I've messed up that, and I have failed to do this, or I shouldn't have said that. You know what the problem is? You're not looking in the right direction. You need to be looking above. You need to be looking toward the Savior. Look to Jesus. Read Hebrews 7:25 with me: "Therefore He [Jesus] is also able to save to the uttermost those who come to God through Him, since He always lives to make intercession for them." Remember who your Savior is! Remember! It says Jesus "lives" to make intercession for us. That's powerful. "He always lives to make intercession for them." Stop looking so much at your failures and start looking to whom you place your confidence: Jesus Christ, the Son of God, the Savior—your Savior.

Let me give you a couple examples of people who either looked at themselves and their wretched sins or looked to Jesus. Take Judas Iscariot as our first example. You know the story. He took thirty pieces of silver to betray Jesus (Matthew 26:14–16). Judas followed that up with betraying Jesus Christ with a kiss (Mark 14:43–45). After that, he hung himself (Matthew 27:3–10). I submit to you that had Judas simply looked to Jesus instead of himself, he would not have had the disastrous end to his life that he had. He could have repented, and God would have forgiven him, but he looked at himself and how he had failed Jesus instead of reaching out to Christ. He realized the foolishness of his actions, but he did not focus on the solution. Judas gave up on himself. He quit. We can do the same when we focus more on our weaknesses versus focusing on our Savior.

Let's look at Peter. Let me direct you to Matthew 14:22–32. Jesus sends His disciples, including Peter, out on a boat in the sea. The evening comes, and so do the wee hours of the morning, specifically between 3:00 a.m. and 6:00 a.m. Jesus walks on the water toward the boat and the disciples are scared, saying, "It is a ghost." In verse 27, Jesus says, "Be of good cheer! It is I; do not be afraid." Then Peter—not any of the other disciples—who said in verse 28, "Lord, if it is You, command me to come to You on the water." Verse 29 reads, "So He said, 'Come.' And when Peter had come down out of the boat, he walked on the water to go to Jesus." You know the rest of the story, but before we get to that, let's state a fact: Peter was the only one of the disciples who had the trust and confidence in Jesus to do something completely illogical to most—to try to walk on water. And, in fact, that's just what he did. Peter walked on the water! I realize he took his eyes off of Jesus and began to notice the danger around him and eventually needed Jesus to bail him out. Still, Peter did what no other man has ever done. He walked on water.

Just after Judas had betrayed Jesus, the troops and officers were going to lead Jesus away. Peter was going to have none of it, and he took his sword and cut the ear off of the high priest's servant, Malchus, whom Jesus promptly healed. Still, Peter was loyal. He loved Jesus, no doubt. However, shortly after this incident something else happened in Peter's life. He failed. This story is recorded in all four Gospels. Let's consider the passage in Luke 22:54–62. Go ahead and put this book down, and read this passage in your own Bible. Then, come back and we'll examine what happened.

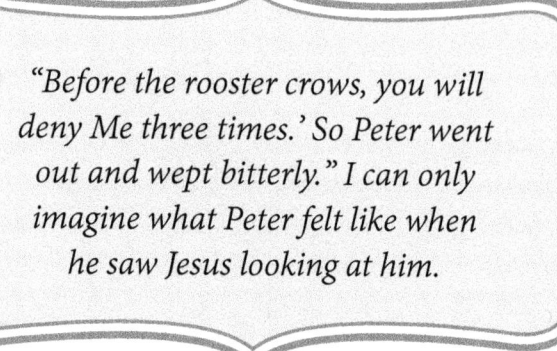

*"Before the rooster crows, you will deny Me three times.' So Peter went out and wept bitterly." I can only imagine what Peter felt like when he saw Jesus looking at him.*

Peter denies even knowing who Jesus is on three occasions, and with each occasion he becomes increasingly firm in his denial. Now, there are times in the Scriptures where you wish you could be a fly on the wall. An extremely powerful moment is about to occur in the life of Peter. After the rooster crowed, as Jesus had predicted, we find these words in Luke 22:61–62, "And the Lord turned and looked at Peter. Then Peter remembered the word of the Lord, how He had said to him, 'Before the rooster crows, you will deny Me three times.' So Peter went out and wept bitterly." I can only imagine what Peter felt like when he saw Jesus looking at him. Maybe it was a look of disappointment from the One he had walked with for some three years since leaving his career as a fisherman. Whatever the look was, along with the realization that He had lied and denied having any relationship with Jesus, it caused Peter to weep bitterly.

## Will I Be Like Judas or Peter?

But you see, that's where the roads divide between Judas and Peter. Judas was disappointed with himself, so he hung himself. Peter was disappointed with himself, but he didn't quit. In fact, let's move forward several weeks from this incident to the Day of Pentecost as recorded in Acts 2. In a relatively short time, Peter had been restored by Jesus, and now he was set to deliver the first gospel sermon. In similar language to when he was in the boat and he was the only one of the disciples to get out of the boat, we find this recorded in Acts 2:14: "But Peter, standing up with the eleven, raised his voice and said to them . . ." Peter moved from denying Christ to delivering a message so powerful—one that proved Jesus was the Son of God convicting the people of their sin—that three thousand believers were baptized that day! That is someone pressing on instead of quitting.

Friends, you are going to fail just like I am going to fail. You are going to be frustrated and maybe say, "How could I be that foolish? What was I thinking?" Do not quit! Do not be a Judas. Being an everyday Christian every single day requires us to keep on keeping on. Remember who your Savior is. He cares about you. He loves you. He spent six hours on the cruel cross for you and now "lives to make intercession" between you and the Father. Stay focused! As the Hebrew writer recorded in Hebrews 12:1–2, ". . . let us run with endurance the race that is set before us, looking unto Jesus, the author and finisher of *our* faith . . ."

**CHALLENGE #10:** ◆◆◆◆◆◆◆

Think deeply—meditate, if you would—day after day on the fact that Jesus is right now your mediator. He is your Advocate and He lives to make intercession for you. Think of that often. Consider how deep His love is for you . . . think about it.

# Chapter 11

# LOOK + LOOK + DO = SUCCESS

I know you remember this spiritual equation. I promised we would be back to it again. We are going to dive a bit deeper into it in this chapter. So, here is James 1:22–25 in its entirety:

> But be doers of the word, and not hearers only, deceiving yourselves. For if anyone is a hearer of the word and not a doer, he is like a man observing his natural face in a mirror; for he observes himself, goes away, and immediately forgets what kind of man he was. But he who looks into the perfect law of liberty and continues *in it*, and is not a forgetful hearer but a doer of the work, this one will be blessed in what he does.

The imagery is fantastic here in James. Suppose you were getting ready for work in the morning or you had to go out and about somewhere. How many of us would go out the door before looking into the mirror? Few, if any, would. Let me share something with you. For some reason, my eyes produce a lot of that goo that sticks in the corners of my eyes. I'm sure it has some scientific term, but for me it's just goo. So, I have to look into the mirror to clean my eyes out. Otherwise, I can't see if I got it all. How will I know if I have goo in my eyes unless I look into the mirror? I won't. I need that mirror to show what I need to correct.

In a similar way, the Bible is our spiritual mirror. How would we possibly know we were doing something contrary to what God would have us to do without His Holy Bible? We couldn't know. That tells me I need to be looking into the Bible, "the perfect law of liberty," to see if what I am doing or not doing is in line with God's commands.

Now, with my eyes, they look fine when I clean them out the first time. But, if I don't clean them out at least one more time before I leave, it will look as if I had not done anything. So, I need to look into the mirror again to make sure I get all of it out the second time. Then, on occasion throughout the day, I'll look in a mirror and be sure there's no more eye goo. Similarly, we cannot expect to just look into the Bible once or even occasionally and expect to remember what we read. There are too many other things competing for our attention. We have to look into it often, over and over again. But, it's not just looking into it, is it? No! We have to do something with the information we have learned. Otherwise, the Bible is of no value to us. We understand that in other areas of life.

> *No! We have to do something with the information we have learned. Otherwise, the Bible is of no value to us.*

Suppose you visit your physician, and she tells you that the cure to your sore is to apply a particular medicine. She tells you that otherwise, the sore could get severely infected and eventually cause serious health problems. If you take that information and do nothing with it, then chances are you will die. The information itself, if not acted upon, has no value.

Let's use a biblical example back in the Old Testament that is very similar to the example I just gave. It is the story of Naaman, found in 2 Kings 5:1–19. It's a fairly long story, but I encourage you to take a couple of minutes and read it. What do we find in this story? Naaman is told what he needed to do (just like when we read our Bibles). Naaman did not particularly like the answer he was given (just like when we see what the Bible says versus what we're doing/not doing). Naaman reasons with Elisha that there has to be a better way. He's not all that interested in Elisha's solution, mainly because the washing in the muddy Jordan River was beneath him.

Let's stop here because many people read their Bibles in a similar way as Naaman. They read what they need to do to live according to God, but they do not particularly like the answer. Maybe it was different than what they were taught before, or it is not what they would prefer to do or not do. Remember how we talked about humility being the bridge that moves us across the finish line from knowing to doing? That's exactly what happened to Naaman. He finally humbled himself thanks to some wise counsel from his servants, which also required humility. We find the result of his obedience in 2 Kings 5:14: "So he went down and dipped seven times in the Jordan, according to the saying of the man of God; and his flesh was restored like the flesh of a little child, and he was clean."

Naaman's will wasn't in line with what he was told to do by God's messenger, Elisha. It was not until he allowed his will to be grafted into God's will that he found success. The same is true for us. We can fight against God's will and His commands. We can ignore them, or we can change them. However, if we ignore them, success does not come our way. Go back to James 1:22 with me. The Bible says that if we are hearers only, then we are "deceiving ourselves." In other words, we are fooling ourselves. You know what it's like to fool yourself because you have done it many times in the past, and you may do it now to some extent.

My wife is fond of telling me when I have new white whiskers in my beard or in my hair. The reality is I am getting older. Now, I could color my beard or hair, which would be fine, but it does not negate the fact that those hairs are really white. In the same way, wearing certain types of clothes may make you look thinner, but it does not fix the issue that you are not thin. Again, there is nothing wrong with wearing these types of clothes, but it does not change the facts. James is telling us by the inspiration of God that if we choose to ignore what God says, and say something like, "Well that doesn't apply to me" or "That commandment isn't that important," then we're just fooling ourselves. Listening and doing what God says is often the road less taken. Jesus spoke of this in Matthew 7:13–14: "Enter by the narrow gate; for wide *is* the gate and broad *is* the way that leads to destruction, and there are many who go in by it. Because narrow *is* the gate and difficult *is* the way which leads to life, and there are few who find it."

In an increasingly evil-loving and evil-promoting world, it is becoming more difficult to listen and to do what the Bible tells us. The world around us is either mocking the Bible's teachings or just ignoring them. Let me remind you, however, that this happened many, many times to people who were trying to live for God. Take Noah, for example. People were not beating down the door to get into the ark. As for the condition of mankind back then? Well, look what we find in Genesis 6:5: "Then the Lord saw that the wickedness of man *was* great in the earth, and *that* every intent of the thoughts of his heart *was* only evil continually."

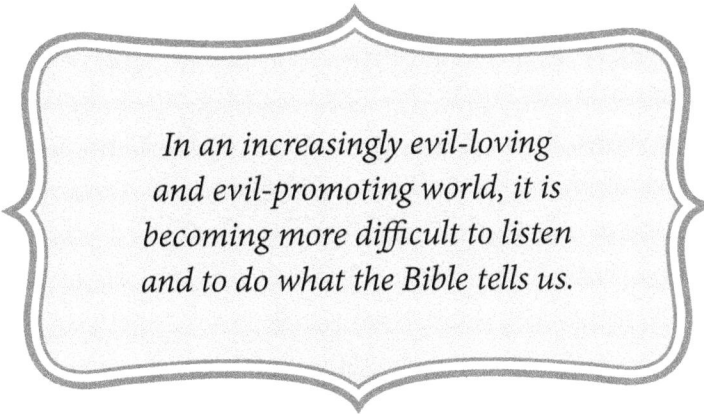

*In an increasingly evil-loving and evil-promoting world, it is becoming more difficult to listen and to do what the Bible tells us.*

Noah's message of repentance fell on deaf ears. Nonetheless, that did not stop Noah from doing what God said and receiving success. Look at the following verses, which show Noah's dedication in spite of what was occurring around him. Genesis 6:22 says, "Thus Noah did; according to all that God commanded him, so he did." In Genesis 7:5 we read, "And Noah did according to all that the Lord commanded him."

LOOK (Listen, in this case) + LOOK (Listen) + DO ("as God commanded") = SUCCESS (Salvation from the flood)

Let's stay in the Old Testament. In Joshua 6 we find the story of the destruction of Jericho. Joshua is, of course, the leader of God's people at this time in history. God tells Joshua in Joshua 6:2, "See! I have given Jericho into your hand, its king, *and* the mighty men of valor." God then proceeds to tell Joshua what the children of Israel are to do. You remember, don't you? They were to march around the city for six consecutive days. On the seventh day, they were to march around the city seven times. To us, that makes no sense. I'm not a military strategist, but I have to think not many who are would plan such an attack. However, that's what God told Joshua. That's not a whole lot different in logic than God telling Noah to build an ark when it had not rained. We can relate to that, can't we? Sometimes God puts us in strange places. Joshua commanded the people to do the following in Joshua 6:10, "You shall not shout or make any noise with your voice, nor shall a word proceed out of your mouth, until the day I say to you 'Shout!'" It is very likely that the people of Jericho would have been mocking the Israelites for what they were doing. Imagine the name-calling that would have taken place. It took discipline to not answer back. It took humility to not do what the Israelites wanted to do but instead to follow the commands of their leader, Joshua, who of course was being led by God. The seventh day comes around, and Joshua tells the people, in 6:16, "Shout, for the LORD has given you the city!"

> *It is very likely that the people of Jericho would have been mocking the Israelites for what they were doing. Imagine the name-calling that would have taken place. It took discipline to not answer back.*

Of course, the result of the shouting and marching is found in Joshua 6:20: "So the people shouted when *the priests* blew the trumpets. And it happened when the people heard the sound of the trumpet, and the people shouted with a great shout, that the wall fell down flat." Let's look at the equation again.

LOOK (Listen to Joshua) + LOOK (Listen to the new commands on the seventh day) + DO (Shout) = SUCCESS (Taking Jericho)

Go ahead and use this equation in story after story of God's people having success. You'll find it fits often. Being an everyday Christian every day requires effort on our part. (We talked about this a little at the beginning of the book.) Notice in the equation that every one of the inputs on the left side requires action. Looking requires effort, as does looking again, and doing naturally requires action. The point is that we will not just accidentally fall into living every day for the Lord. The path of least resistance is the wide way. As Jesus said in Matthew 7:14, "... narrow *is* the gate, and difficult *is* the way which leads to life, and there are few who find it." We have to find it. We have to seek the Christian life. We have to want it. We have to put in the effort for it. But, if we're willing to put in the effort to live the Christian life, oh, what a wonderful life it is.

## CHALLENGE #11: ♦♦♦♦♦♦♦

When you sin, when I sin, something has gone wrong on the left-hand side of the equation. Either we don't know what to do (LOOK), or we've forgotten what to do (LOOK), or we've just chosen not to do what's right (DO), which I would say more times than not comes from a lack of humbling ourselves under God's commands. So, think about the last time you knowingly sinned. What went wrong?

# Chapter 12

# Everyday Christianity— The Extraordinary Life

Jesus said, in John 10:10, "I have come that they may have life, and that they may have *it* more abundantly." The verse may specifically refer more to eternal life, but it is absolutely applicable to our lives every single day as Christians. Brothers and sisters in Christ, we have the abundant life! There is no greater life you can live in this wonderful world than the Christian life. Paul, when comparing his old life with the new life in Christ, wrote in Philippians 3:7-8, "But what things were gain to me, these I have counted loss for Christ. Yet indeed I also count all things loss for the excellence of the knowledge of Christ Jesus my Lord, for whom I have suffered the loss of all things, and count them as rubbish, that I may gain Christ..."

The apostle Paul gave up practically everything he had when he became a Christian: power, influence, fame, and likely wealth. Still, he considered all his accomplishments and all that he had worked for as of no value when compared to a life in Christ. Paul understood just how abundant a life in Christ was. What we have in an abundant life is a relationship with the Son of God, who is our Mediator and our Savior, who went to the cross for each of us and became the ransom for our sins. It is because of that we have the promise of heaven, and it is that promise that provides us with the "peace that passes understanding" regardless of our lot in life or circumstances we face. That, my friends, is worth more than all the gold, silver, and money in the world. That is the abundant life.

Do you realize how many people are seeking the abundant life? They attempt to create the "abundance" through money, influence, family, or fame when the abundant life is right under their noses . . . a life with Jesus Christ.

Listen to what the apostle John has told us in 1 John 5:11–13, "And this is the testimony: that God has given us eternal life, and this life is in His Son. He who has the Son has life; he who does not have the Son of God does not have life. These things I have written to you who believe in the name of the Son of God, that you may know that you have eternal life . . ." According to John, the Christian should not walk around wondering if he will make it into heaven. Brothers and sisters, do you realize how powerful that is? Do you realize how powerful that is for your state of mind, for your priorities in your life, for the stress of life, when you know that you have a better place waiting? You have a home in heaven with God, with Jesus, and with the saints who have gone on before you. There is absolutely nothing I would exchange for that! There is no amount of money, number of friendships, or anything else that can give that type of peace. Every single Christian has the ability to have that certainty of heaven.

## Alive and Confident In Christ

How is that possible? John addresses that earlier in the same book. In 1 John 1:7, we find, "But if we walk in the light as He is in the light, we have fellowship with one another, and the blood of Jesus Christ His Son cleanses us from all sin." Did you hear that? If we walk in the light as He is in the light, then your sins are gone, wiped clean. The promise of eternal life in heaven motivates me to walk in the light. I want to walk in the brightest of lights. I want to surround myself with godly thoughts. I want to sing those beautiful hymns not just on Sunday but throughout the week. I want to be in contact throughout the day in prayer. I cannot get enough of Jesus in my life. I cannot get enough of the Father. I cannot read my Bible enough. I just want to drink deeply every ounce of love God has shown to me in His Word.

> *The promise of eternal life in heaven motivates me to walk in the light. I want to walk in the brightest of lights.*

Let's take a look at a passage in Ephesians. We touched on this chapter earlier in the book, but I want you to look at Ephesians 2:1–2 with me, "And you *He made alive*, who were dead in trespasses and sins, in which you once walked according to the course of this world . . ." What does that tell me? It tells me that the people of this world who are engulfed in sin are essentially "dead," and I, along with you, were once in that camp. But as Christians, Paul said that God has made us "alive"! We are not dead to sin, but we are alive in Christ Jesus! To God be the glory! If that doesn't bring you joy and peace, I just don't know what would.

Paul said something similar in 1 Corinthians 6:9–11 that we referenced earlier. Paul gives a long list of sins that characterize the unrighteous. Then he says in verse 11, "And such were some of you. But you were washed, but you were sanctified, but you were justified in the name of the Lord Jesus and by the Spirit of our God."

I am no different. You are no different. Sure, we may not have engaged in these specific sins, or perhaps we have. However, if we have repented of our sins and have been washed in the blood of Jesus, we have been sanctified. We have been justified, and praise the Lord for that!

Let me say this. I don't know what your prayer life is like. I suspect that most of us pray when we lay our heads down for sleep. It does not get any better than being able to say to our Father in our final thoughts before we drift to sleep, "Father in heaven, thank you for the forgiveness of sins; thank you for salvation; thank you for the promise of heaven." When we can lay our heads down in sleep knowing that we have a place in heaven reserved for us, that brings a level of tranquility that no amount of money or possessions could buy. Recall the words of the apostle Paul in Romans 8:18, "For I consider that the sufferings of this present time are not worthy *to be compared* with the glory which shall be revealed in us." "No comparison," says Paul.

## God Is with You, Even When . . .

Now, let me say I know life is not wonderful all the time. There are failures in our careers. There are problems in our families. There is sickness and disease that take our loved ones far earlier than expected or in ways we would not have imagined. We experience disappointments and regrets from things we've done or failed to do. These things, and a host of others, cause pain, anguish, and disappointment. Press on, though. As Paul said, these "sufferings . . . are not worthy to be compared with the glory." But, let me remind you further of why yours is an extraordinarily abundant life. No matter the woes and difficulties you face, you have this promise found in 1 Peter 3:12, "For the eyes of the LORD *are* on the righteous, and His ears *are open* to their prayers..."

Again, let me remind you. You are able to speak directly to the One who made the universe. He made you. He knows everything about you, far more than you know. He knows what makes you joyful and what makes you sad. He knows what is troubling you now and He holds the future in His hand. And, you get to speak to Him. Is that not awesome? Meditate on that thought for just a moment. Think of the incredible privilege you have to speak directly with Almighty God in heaven. Then there is the promise found in Romans 8:38–39 regarding God's love for us, "For I am persuaded that neither death nor life, nor angels nor principalities nor powers, nor things present nor things to come, nor height nor depth, nor any other created thing, shall be able to separate us from the love of God which is in Christ Jesus our Lord."

> *You are able to speak directly to the One who made the universe. He made you. He knows everything about you, far more than you know. He knows what makes you joyful and what makes you sad.*

God loves you. God loves you. God loves you! Please don't ever forget that. Please don't every question that. Please don't let that escape from your mind any day of your life. God loved you enough to make the supreme sacrifice of giving his Son on the cross. If he did that, he surely isn't going to abandon you now. He loves you. As the psalmist questioned in Psalms 116:12, "What shall I render to the Lord *for* all His benefits toward me?" The answer is everything. Look at what God has given you on this earth. Look at the untold blessings you have regardless of your current circumstance, good or bad. You are a blood-bought child of the living God.

All He wants from you is your life. Jesus said just that in Matthew 16:24–26.

> If anyone desires to come after Me, let him deny himself, and take up his cross, and follow Me. For whoever desires to save his life will lose it, but whoever loses his life for My sake will find it. For what profit is it to a man if he gains the whole world and loses his own soul? Or what will a man give in exchange for his soul?

Given what He has done for you, the untold blessings, forgiveness of sins, salvation for eternity, how can I give him anything else than my life of dedication to Him?

The apostle Paul spoke of this life in Galatians 2:20 when he wrote, "I have been crucified with Christ; it is no longer I who live, but Christ lives in me; and the *life* which I now live in the flesh I live by faith in the Son of God, who loved me and gave Himself for me." The same should be true for us. Our lives belong to God. We owe Him everything, and without Him we would have nothing, and we would be nothing. There would be no forgiveness of sins and no promise of Heaven.

After all God has given us, how can we not give our very lives in service to Him and in dedication to Him?

**CHALLENGE #12:** ❖❖❖❖❖❖❖

Count your blessings. Really, I want to challenge you to count your blessings... all of them. Years ago I was teaching a high school class and we did just this and filled an entire, enormous chalkboard. So, go ahead and list any and everything with which God has blessed you. Spend plenty of time on it. You will be amazed when you stop and seriously think about what all God has given to you.

## Chapter 13

# It Will Be Worth It All

Imagine you planned a vacation with family members from around the country to somewhere you had always wanted to visit, or perhaps you planned a get-together with friends you had not seen in years. Maybe you were going to see people who you had literally served in battle with or people who you played with on a memorable sports team. You spent hours after hours planning for it, leaving no stone unturned. The anticipation grew as the day approached. Perhaps you sat around and daydreamed about what conversations would be like when you were together again. You wondered what you would do first, or with whom you wanted to sit down and talk. You made sure your bags were packed, plane tickets were in hand, and directions had been finalized to the destination. When you finally arrived, what you enjoyed was even greater than anticipated. How great it was! Perhaps the visit with friends was even more fun than you thought it would be, or the place you were visiting turned out to be more beautiful than you could have imagined.

Regardless of how great that time may have been, let me tell you . . . that feeling is the tiniest of a drop in the bucket compared to what it will be like when Jesus says to you and to me, "Come, you blessed of My Father, inherit the kingdom prepared for you from the foundation of the world . . ." (Matt. 25:34). There will be celebrations like there have never been before. There will be shouts of joy like none have ever heard and hugs like none before them. Oh, there's a great day coming! There's a great day coming for those who are in Christ Jesus. It will be magnificent! Hebrews 9:28 tells us, "To those who eagerly wait for Him He will appear a second time, apart from sin, for salvation." I'm eagerly waiting for Him. Jesus is coming soon. I don't know when, nor does anyone else who has ever lived on this earth. What I do know, though, is He is coming, and I must be ready for that day.

## That Glorious Day

The apostle Paul gave us a glimpse into that day. He was writing to the Christians in Thessalonica. Many there thought the coming of Christ was imminent. They were afraid that some among them who had passed away were going to miss out on the Day of the Lord. Not so, said Paul. In 1 Thessalonians 4:15–18 Paul wrote,

> For this we say to you by the word of the Lord, that we who are alive *and* remain until the coming of the Lord will by no means precede those who are asleep. For the Lord Himself will descend from heaven with a shout, with the voice of an archangel, and with the trumpet of God. And the dead in Christ will rise first. Then we who are alive *and* remain shall be caught up together with them in the clouds to meet the Lord in the air. And thus we shall always be with the Lord. Therefore comfort one another with these words.

The view we have of that glorious day is remarkable. The shout, the trumpet, the fact that the dead will be first is quite a scene and one we wait for with great anticipation. It will be the greatest event the world has ever seen, and it will close out the existence of this old world. As magnificent as the scene clearly will be, there is a phrase in that passage that makes me cry, "And thus we shall always be with the Lord." That's it. It doesn't get any better than that.

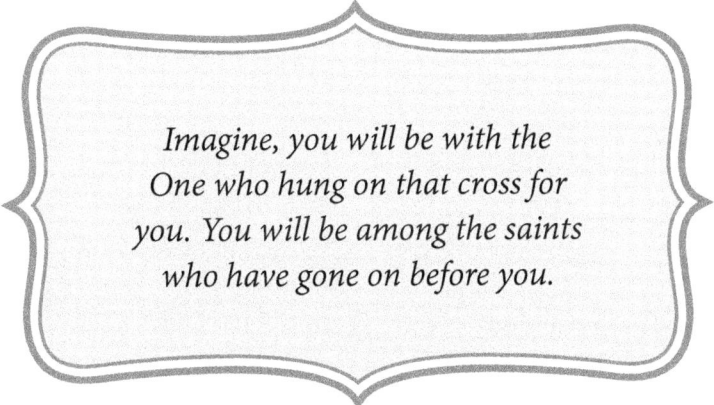

*Imagine, you will be with the One who hung on that cross for you. You will be among the saints who have gone on before you.*

Let me tell you why it does not get any better. Separation hurts. Some of you know that more than others. I hate it when I'm away from my wife and kids. I mean it. I've been away from them for a week before, and I count the hours until I see them again. But, for some of you, you've lost your spouse or even your children. I can't imagine either. That separation hurts exponentially more than being away from my family. Once that glorious day comes, however, you and I will no longer be separated from the faithful loved ones who have gone before us. But, more than that you will no longer be separated from the God you love or the Son you love. No longer will you wonder what He is like. You will dwell with Him forever, never to be separated. We will always be with the Lord. Imagine, you will be with the One who hung on that cross for you. You will be among the saints who have gone on before you. There you will be with the apostles—Paul, Peter, and John and the others—who paved the way for you to enter into heaven. You will be able to look and see Stephen, the first Christian martyr. There you will be with others who, like you, diligently served their Lord. Again, never to be separated.

In the book of Revelation, John gives us a look inside heaven. In 21:4, John writes, "And God will wipe away every tear from their eyes; there shall be no more death, nor sorrow, nor crying. There shall be no more pain, for the former things have passed away." Did you hear that? Any and everything that has ever caused you one ounce of pain or sorrow on earth will not be present in heaven. Nothing! No pain, death, or sorrow. They will all be gone, never to be seen again. That motivates me. I want to be there. That is the place for me. Just the shear absence of pain and sorrow would be enough. I would take that, no questions asked. Even if God told me heaven was not hell, I would be satisfied. Indeed, more than satisfied.

But, God has given us so much more than just the absence of pain and sorrow. I love the description John gives us of heaven in 21:23, 25: "The city had no need of the sun or of the moon to shine in it, for the glory of God illuminated it. The Lamb *is* its light. . . . Its gates shall not be shut at all by day (there shall be no night there)."

When I think of the constant light and (I love this next one and the gospel song based on it) the fact that gates shall not be shut, it brings to mind the idea of perfect, complete safety and satisfaction. The dark often scares us; darkness is where evil lurks.

However, in heaven we will have nothing to fear again. We will have nothing to bring worry into our hearts. We will never again be threatened. We will have complete peace. John says in Revelation 21:27, "But there shall by no means enter it anything that defiles, or causes an abomination or a lie, but only those who are written in the Lamb's Book of Life." Peter describes heaven in 1 Peter 1:4 as "an inheritance incorruptible and undefiled and that does not fade away, reserved in heaven for you . . ." Nothing will deteriorate in heaven. Everything deteriorates on earth. Everything eventually breaks down, including each of us. Not so in heaven. Day 1,000,000 in heaven (if there will even be days) will be no less great than day 1. All those days, months, years, and decades you might have struggled on earth will be worth it all for an eternal home with God, Jesus, and the saints.

> *Nothing will deteriorate in heaven. Everything deteriorates on earth. Everything eventually breaks down, including each of us. Not so in heaven.*

## Eternal Preparation Is Underway

Remember, Jesus is preparing a place for you. The Master and Savior is getting your place in heaven ready for you. In John 14:2–4, Jesus says, "In My Father's house are many mansions; if *it* were not so, I would have told you. I go to prepare a place for you. And if I go and prepare a place for you, I will come again and receive you to Myself; that where I am, *there* you may be also." I sit here and read those verses and I am in awe—awe at the monumental amount of love seen in these words from the Son of Man, the Prince of Peace.

Look at the words He closes with: "that where I am, there you may be also."

I want that. I want all of that. I want the mansion. I want to be with Jesus. I want to live in that place that is incorruptible, where there is no evil, where there is no sorrow, and no tears. I want to be with the saints who have gone on before me. I want to be in that place with the streets of gold and whose beauty will far surpass anything on this earth. That is the place that I want. No, that is the place that I am planning to be for an eternity. Because of that and these magnificent promises and glimpses into heaven, I am going to live every single day for Christ. I am going to be an everyday Christian every single day. I am going to love God, love others, serve God, serve others, pray fervently, and walk in the light as he is in the light. Nothing is going to stop me because nothing is worth missing heaven—absolutely nothing!

> *I want to be with Jesus. I want to live in that place that is incorruptible, where there is no evil, where there is no sorrow, and no tears.*

Let's finish our journey in living as an everyday Christian every single day by looking at some words from the final chapter in the Bible. In Revelation 22:7, 12, Jesus said, "Behold, I am coming quickly.... And behold, I am coming quickly, and My reward *is* with Me, to give to every one according to his work." We don't know when He is coming. It may be morning, noon, or night. Because we don't know when He is coming, we must always be ready to meet our Lord and Savior.

You and I have a reward. It will be greater than any reward you could ever hope to have on this earth. Let me leave you with just a few closing thoughts. Don't give up. If you're fortunate, you may live eighty, ninety, or more years on this earth. Regardless, that is nothing compared to eternity. Stay focused on Christ. Stay motivated to serve God and those around you. The reward is great. If I don't see you here on earth, let's meet in heaven. I'm planning on being there, and I hope you are too. Be an everyday Christian every day, and we will spend all of eternity in heaven together with Almighty God and our Savior Jesus Christ.

## CHALLENGE #13: ❯❯❯❯❯❯❯

Live every day for Christ. Seek those things above and make it your undivided number-one purpose to be in heaven for eternity!

www.ingramcontent.com/pod-product-compliance
Lightning Source LLC
Chambersburg PA
CBHW061802070526
44586CB00023B/2677